PAtg 86-B17268

CONTEMPORARY
CHORAL
ARRANGING

CONTEMPORARY CHORAL ARRANGING

Arthur E. Ostrander

Dana Wilson

School of Music, Ithaca College

Prentice-Hall   Englewood Cliffs, N.J. 07632

Library of Congress Cataloging-in-Publication Data

OSTRANDER, ARTHUR E. (date)
  Contemporary choral arranging.

  Includes index.
  1. Arrangement (Music)   2. Choral music.
I. Wilson, Dana.   II. Title.
MT70.5.087 1986   784.1′0028   85-17000
ISBN 0-13-169756-0

Editorial/production supervision and
  interior design by Eva Jaunzems
Cover design by 20/20 Services, Inc.
Manufacturing buyer: Ray Keating

Printed in the United States of America

10   9   8   7   6   5   4   3   2   1

0-13-169756-0   01

Prentice-Hall International (UK) Limited, *London*
Prentice-Hall of Australia Pty. Limited, *Sydney*
Prentice-Hall Canada Inc., *Toronto*
Prentice-Hall Hispanoamericana, S.A., *Mexico*
Prentice-Hall of India Private Limited, *New Delhi*
Prentice-Hall of Japan, Inc., *Tokyo*
Prentice-Hall of Southeast Asia Pte. Ltd., *Singapore*
Editora Prentice-Hall do Brasil, Ltda., *Rio de Janeiro*
Whitehall Books Limited, *Wellington, New Zealand*

To our wives
Carrie and Elisabeth

CONTENTS

8

PLANNING THE ARRANGEMENT   115

Initial Considerations Regarding Performance Group and Musical Source   115

Detailed Study of the Musical Source   116
Text 116, Melodic Form 116, Pitch and Rhythmic Organization 117

Planning the Overall Form of the Arrangement   117
Sectional (AABA) 117, Strophic 118, Strophic with Refrain 118

The Contribution of Musical Elements to Form Delineation   118
Texture 118, Accompaniment 119, Dynamics 119, Key 119, Tempo 119

Application of Musical Elements to Specific Forms   119
Sectional (AABA) 119, Strophic 120, Strophic with Refrain 120

Adding Introductions and Endings   121

Final Assembly of the Arrangement   121

Applying the Planning Progression to an Existing Arrangement   121
Considering the Type of Group 121, Detailed Study of the Musical Source and Text 122, Planning the Overall Form of the Arrangement 122, Summary of Formal Treatment 123, Adding Introductions and Endings 123

9

THREE-PART ARRANGING   124

Typical Voice Combinations and Applications   124

Homophonic Textures   125
Note-against-Note 125, Animated Homophony 127, Melody Line with Background Vocal Texture 130

12

ADAPTING AN EXISTING ARRANGEMENT TO A DIFFERENT CHORAL COMBINATION

13

JAZZ VOCAL STYLES

14

COUNTRY, ROCK, AND POP VOCAL STYLES

ACKNOWLEDGMENTS

Our first debt is to Bowdoin College, where as undergraduates we both sang in, and wrote for, vocal ensembles. That experience was the practical basis for our understanding of, and interest in, choral arranging.

The many illustrative examples throughout the book demonstrate the talent and craft of a host of professional arrangers to whom we are indebted. They have helped to establish, confirm, and enhance the styles and techniques discussed in this book, and, over the years, have presented effective and exciting choral music to the public. We also thank them and their publishers for granting permission to reprint arrangement excerpts.

Several people assisted in this project. Eva Jaunzems, our editor, was most helpful in her guidance and suggestions in each phase of the publication process. Special thanks are also extended to Dorothy Owens for her help in the preparation of the manuscript and to Dorothy Ostrander for handling the detailed correspondence with the publishers.

Finally, we wish to thank the students in our choral arranging courses, who have helped shape the content and direction of this book, and to express our appreciation for the support of our colleagues at Ithaca College, particularly to David Riley, who provided insight and information.

A.E.O.
D.W.

CHAPTER ONE

INTRODUCTION

CHORAL ARRANGING IS A CREATIVE PROCESS that develops a source melody and text into a complete setting for a particular choral combination with accompaniment. This book provides the framework for developing choral arranging ability in a logical series of chapters devoted to acquiring technical skills in various aspects of writing, with a view toward incorporating these techniques in the overall creation of a unified work.

This approach to arranging can be used either in individual study or in the context of a formal course. The developing professional arranger, the church or community choir director, and the school vocal teacher are good examples of individuals who can use this book. Teachers of traditional choral arranging or vocal jazz and popular arranging can also use this book as the pedagogical basis for courses devoted to these topics.

This book assumes an understanding of basic harmonic and melodic organization in music. Chapters 2 and 3 present a review of all the pertinent basic musical information needed to successfully master the arranging concepts presented in subsequent chapters, but the reader should approach these initial review chapters with enough previous musical experience to feel comfortable in applying these concepts to new possibilities in writing for voices. In addition, the potential arranger should be familiar with various styles of choral writing from a background of hearing and performing choral music.

One of the unique strengths of this book is the attention given in the later chapters to jazz and other popular styles. Vocal jazz and show choirs are burgeoning in this country, and there is a need for good arrangers—both professional and amateur—in these areas. The relevant chapters are designed, first, to acquaint the arranger who is not familiar technically with jazz, rock, country, and pop music with their primary components and arranging techniques; second, to familiarize the instrumental jazz arranger with various approaches to choral writing. Practical applications range from writing for radio and TV jingles to arranging in the combinations and styles of various popular contemporary vocal groups. This book fosters the principle that a choral arrangement, whether in a traditional, sacred, or popular (jazz, rock, country, etc.) style, must exhibit stylistic consistency throughout.

This book approaches arranging from the perspective of creating a musical setting for an existing source melody rather than of composing choral music. Toward this end, many musical excerpts in a variety of musical styles from current choral arrangements are included in the text. This allows the reader to confirm comprehension of theoretical arranging concepts through study of current choral literature arranged by established figures in the field. A number of complete choral arrangements in various styles and voice combinations are also included in Appendix II to allow detailed study of arranging techniques extended over the course of an entire composition. These pieces are analyzed in detail at the end of chapters devoted to arranging techniques in a particular style or voice combination.

An individual can only learn choral arranging by actively working with musical materials. To this end, exercises are included at the end of many chapters. Each exercise focuses on central arranging concepts from the chapter as they apply to a particular source melody (the source melodies along with other appropriate melodies in a variety of styles appear in Appendix I). These exercises are intended not only for the teacher to assign in a formal class context but also for the individual to complete as a means of gathering skill in the craft of choral writing. Through continued practice in short exercises, the once seemingly insurmountable task of putting together a complete choral arrangement can become the skillful piecing together of short sections that it is in reality.

Nothing is more important for the choral arranger than the experience of singing in a choral ensemble. Here the arranger can gain practical knowledge not only of voice ranges and timbres but also of the way in which range and tessitura, as well as dynamics and other factors, effect the manner in which voice parts are able to combine. It also follows that extended exercises and arrangements should be performed by a choral group if at all possible to give the arranger the immediate benefit of hearing how they sound. Nothing can teach the practical lesson of what ''works'' better than hearing the live performance of an arrangement.

It is hoped that this book will help to stimulate the individual's interest in developing and refining the craft, as well as to enhance the appreciation of the art of choral arranging.

CHAPTER TWO

INITIAL CHORAL ARRANGING CONSIDERATIONS

THIS CHAPTER DEALS WITH THE THREE TECHNICAL ASPECTS of choral arranging: the capabilities of the human voice, scoring and notation, and text setting. While the first will be discussed in some detail, there is no substitute for hearing firsthand the various voice types in different registers and their interaction in a choral setting. Proper and clear notation is crucial to a good performance, regardless of the difficulty of the arrangement. Since the primary consideration of the music is to enhance the meaning of the words, the text must be set properly in order that its comprehensibility be best projected.

VOICE TYPES AND COMBINATIONS ACCORDING TO AGE GROUPS

Elementary School Level

Arrangements for young children have one or two vocal parts. The two parts are both notated in treble clef, designated I and II rather than soprano and alto, because the ranges are somewhat limited; and boys, as well as girls, may be singing both parts. The range for each is basically the same, although I stays rather consistently above II in the arrangement:

So as not to tire the voices, the *tessitura*—the register in which most of the part
'lies—should fall near the middle of the range.

Due to limited pitch control, reading ability, concentration, and rehearsal time,
the vocal writing for most elementary school-level groups should be basically
stepwise and diatonic, and the lines should consist of short phrases separated by
rests for frequent breaths. Rhythms should also be simple, although short, syncopated phrases are usually accessible, especially when reinforced by the accompaniment. Arrangements for this level are usually accompanied by piano, although the
addition of a hand drum, tambourine, or hand-clapping can add a nice dimension
if appropriate to the material.

Middle School Level

At the next school level—grades 6 to 8 or 9, often referred to as the middle
school level—boys' voices begin to change to the mature low voice. Until recently,
a chorus at this level would often sing music for sopranos, altos, and baritones,
with the boys whose voices had not changed singing the alto part along with the
lower-voiced girls, and those whose voices had changed singing baritone—a com-
promise between tenor and bass. Because these categorizations are generally un-
satisfactory musically and socially, the *cambiata*, or changing voice, has been
introduced for the boys whose voices have not yet deepened.

The comfortable range for the cambiata voice is a to a^1, with the possible
extremes f to c^2:

The part is written (where it sounds) in treble clef.

The boys whose voices have already changed sing the baritone part in bass
clef, with the range $B\flat$ to $e\flat^1$:

By the middle school grades, girls' voices are maturing into higher or lower
women's voices, though there are rarely true altos yet. Therefore, while there are
some arrangements designated soprano-alto-cambiata-baritone, the most common
combinations are soprano I-soprano II-cambiata-baritone, or soprano-cambiata-bar-
itone. Very practical ranges for the girls' parts are:

The parts can be more independent than they are in elementary school-level
arrangements, but doubling is quite common. Because the boys' voices are in
transition at this age and often lack focus and security, the baritone and, even more,

the cambiata parts should be predominantly stepwise. The cambiata will often take turns doubling the baritone or soprano II parts, having its own notes primarily in homophonic passages.

If the girls' parts share text and rhythm, they may be placed on the same staff.

High School Level

The common voice combination at the high school level is soprano-alto-tenor-bass (SATB). The ranges are:

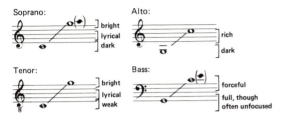

The reader will note, for the purposes of quick memorization, that the range of the soprano and tenor is $c–g$, while that of the altos and basses is the opposite—$g–c$. These ranges are a rule of thumb—for example, some tenor sections cannot produce a solid high g^1, while some bass sections can sing a nice, round high d^1.

As mentioned earlier, of greatest importance is the fact that the tessitura of any part must not be in either extreme end of the range, as the voice tires quickly in extreme registers. Furthermore, the arranger should become familiar with the tone quality of each voice in various registers in order to control the balance and color and to create the desired musical effect.

Sometimes a choir has many more women than men. A very popular solution is to arrange for soprano-alto-baritone (SAB), thereby grouping all the men together on a baritone part whose range is still essentially A to d^1. This solves the balance problem but denies the men the satisfaction of exploring the brilliant high notes in the case of a tenor and the rich low notes in the case of a bass. These colorful registers, of course, are also lost in an SAB arrangement, and so the combination should be used only when necessary.

Mature Adult Voices

After puberty, a maturing voice does not naturally extend its range very much, but rather its sound becomes more focused and consistent throughout its range. However, as the extremes become more secure, the arranger can write (sparingly!) a note a major second above or below the ranges given for the respective high school voice categories. The soprano range thus becomes $b\flat$ to a^2, and so forth.

Greater security and focus also bring clarity to the choir section, which, in turn, permits faster lines and more complex vocal textures. The key to writing an effective arrangement employing the full spectrum of the choral ranges and colors, however, is still to gear it to a specific type of chorus: a madrigal group is accustomed to intricate textures and solo passages, a jazz choir to complex rhythmic relationships and soloistic writing, a barbershop group to *a cappella* arrangements, and so forth. At a more practical level, a good college choir that rehearses three times per week can generally perform a more demanding arrangement than can a church choir that meets one evening a week to prepare the music for the following service.

MUSICAL NOTATION

Correct notation is important for three reasons: first for clarity—so that the arranger's musical intentions are best communicated to the performer; second, for a positive psychological effect on the performer—the notation being the first indication to the performer of the arranger's expertise; third, for ease of performance—contributing to a more efficient rehearsal and successful concert. This discussion will focus upon the most common issues concerning choral arranging.

Score Setup

Generally, there should be one staff for each vocal part, and each staff should be identified ("Soprano," "I," or the like) at the beginning of the arrangement and, any time the format changes, in the left-hand margin. The text is written beneath its respective staff. Soprano and alto parts are written in treble clef; the tenor part is written in treble clef, though it sounds one octave below; the bass and baritone parts are written in bass clef (Ex. 2–1). This is referred to as "open scoring." Note that the vocal staves are linked to each other only by a vertical line in the left-hand margin to indicate that all parts sound simultaneously. Bar lines, however, are not joined together from part to part, even in the right-hand margin.

When the female parts or male parts share the same text and approximately the same rhythms, both parts (soprano and alto, or tenor and bass) may share the same staff to save space. (This means, of course, that the tenor part would have to be written in bass clef—at the pitch where it sounds—along with the bass part.) If needed to distinguish the vocal parts, the upper voice's note stems should go up, while those of the lower voice should go down (Ex. 2–2). This two-stave setup is referred to as "close scoring." If close scoring is used at all, it must be used for an entire section of the arrangement, as switching back and forth between this and open scoring described above can be very confusing to the performer. Note in measure 3 of the above example that the sopranos have a different text and rhythm from those of the altos. For this very brief passage, the soprano text can be above the staff for clarity. Should this continue, however, such notation becomes awkward and open scoring should be used.

When a vocal soloist is featured against a choral background, it is best to put his or her part on a separate staff above all of the choral parts. However, a tenor solo, for example, may be kept on the tenors' staff if (a) the rest of the tenors are not singing, in which case the designation "solo" above the staff is sufficient to

Example 2–1. Open score setup. Foster (arr. M. Hayes): *Some Folks*

indicate the solo passage; or (b) the solo is merely a brief interaction with the choral tenors, where "stems up" distinguish the solo part from the "stems down" of the rest.

Dynamic markings are placed above each vocal staff, so as not to be confused with the text, which is written beneath the staff. Tempo indications are placed only above the top vocal part and the instrumental accompaniment.

Occasionally, singers are asked to speak, shout, clap, or make some other gesture of unspecified pitch. In this case the symbol " ♩ " replaces the conventional

Example 2–2. Close scoring. Spence, Keith, and Bergman (arr. D. Riley and D. Wilson): *Nice 'n' Easy* (Accompaniment omitted.)

note (thus indicating specific rhythm, but not pitch), with specific instructions as to what is desired.

A piano accompaniment is linked to the vocal parts only by the vertical line at the left-hand end of the staves. A double line, or *brace*, is then drawn to connect the vocal parts and separate them visually from the accompaniment, while the piano part is bracketed in the margin and the bar lines of its two staves are connected vertically. Treble and bass clef are used on the respective piano staves, unless both hands are playing in the treble or bass register. Dynamics markings are placed between the staves unless those of the treble staff differ from those of the bass staff, in which case the dynamic markings are placed beneath the respective staves (refer back to Example 2–1).

Sometimes a piano part which merely duplicates the vocal parts is added to the score of an *a cappella* arrangement to aid in learning parts. In this case, "for rehearsal only" is written at the beginning, between the staves of the piano part, to ensure that the piano is not played in performance.

An organ accompaniment is notated in the same manner as that of the piano. If there is a rather active pedal part, a third staff in bass clef is added below the keyboard staves and is connected to them by the left-hand margin line but not by the bracket.

When other instruments are involved, the left-hand margin extends to include their staves. Arrangements of sacred music sometimes employ a brass or string ensemble. Both are usually placed in the score above the choral parts, even though a keyboard part in the same arrangement is placed beneath the choral parts. In brass quintet writing, the two trumpets usually share the top staff, the horn part is written on the next staff, and the trombone and tuba share the third staff. In the more common quartet writing, the two staves are shared by two trumpets and two trombones, respectively (Ex. 2–3).

String parts, too, are placed above the choral parts in the score (unlike the setup of an orchestral score that includes choral parts). An arrangement may include any number of strings, from a solo violin to a full string orchestra, and the reader is urged to consult an orchestration book regarding string notation and techniques.

Vocal jazz arrangements usually employ a rhythm section (piano or guitar, string or electric bass, and drum set) and often three wind instruments such as trumpet, saxophone, and trombone. All of these are placed beneath the choral parts in the score as follows:

(choral parts)

winds

piano/guitar

bass

drums

Guitar parts are written in treble clef sounding an octave below, while string and electric bass parts are written in bass clef sounding an octave below. Unpitched

Example 2–3. F. Handel (arr. W. Pelz): *Joy to the World*

percussion such as drums uses a neutral clef and often just a one-line staff. Chapter 15 discusses in detail writing for the instruments of the vocal jazz ensemble.

It should be mentioned that in rather simple arrangements where saving space is important (to minimize printing costs, for example), it is possible to use verbal instructions such as: ''Flute may double piano treble clef part on repeat.''

The key signature should occur at the beginning of each system of the arrangement, just to the right of the clef sign. Should the key signature change within the arrangement, the new signature must be preceded by double bar lines. If the new signature essentially cancels all sharps or flats, natural signs are used to so indicate. Should a key signature change at the beginning of a system, the change should also be indicated at the end of the previous system to prepare the performer for the change (Ex. 2–4).

The meter (time) signature is placed on each staff at the beginning of an arrangement just to the right of the key signature. The meter signature should not recur unless the meter changes, in which case it should again be placed on each

Example 2–4.

I've   nev - er been to the   moon —   and I don't think I'll   go   I've

nev - er been to the   moon — *(etc.)*

staff of the system preceded only by a single bar line (see Example 2–4 above). As in the case of the key change, should a meter change occur at the beginning of a system, it should also be indicated at the end of the previous system.

Because arrangements often involve sections which recur exactly, there are a few common notational practices with regard to form. The repeat signs symbolized by ‖: :‖ indicate that the section between these markings is to be repeated, regardless of length.

The arranger may desire to repeat a section, with different endings for each repeat. Thus, different endings are written, as in Example 2–5.

Example 2–5. A repeated section with different endings.

I'll   love   you for - ev - er   I'll   I'll nev - er   let you   go ——

Note that double bar lines signal the beginning of this device and that the repeat sign occurs at the end of the first ending. A bracket extends above each part to clearly indicate each ending. As many endings as needed for section repetition are possible, all but the last ending having a repeat sign.

If the performer is to return to the very beginning of the arrangement for the repeat, no left repeat sign ‖: is necessary at the beginning; the absence of that marking dictates that the performer return to the beginning.

Frequently a section is not to be repeated, but the performer is to return to an earlier section. The term *Da Capo (D.C.)* directs the performer back to the beginning, while *Dal Segno (D.S.)* directs the performer to an earlier place within the arrangement where the sign 𝄋 has been placed above all parts.

From there the piece may end in the middle of the score at a point marked *fine* (pronounced "feenay"). If the performer is to move from a section previously sung to an entirely separate section to end the arrangement, a coda sign, symbolized by ⊕, is placed above the parts at the point where the performer must jump to the coda, identified by "coda" or another ⊕ marking and often clearly separate from the rest of the arrangement. The *D.C.* or *D.S.* should in that case have been followed by *al coda* to prepare this move (Ex. 2–6).

Example 2–6. Sing the first line;
return to the sign 𝄋 and sing to the
coda symbol ⊕ ; then jump to the
coda and finish the arrangement.

D.S. al Coda

These conventional devices save space and writing time. They do, however, present a certain performance risk, since a singer might forget to repeat or jump to the coda. Furthermore, if the singers read during performance, a certain amount of page-flipping is inevitable. The arranger must weigh all of these factors when setting up the score.

Chord Nomenclature

Only music in which some degree of improvisation is expected in performance uses chord symbols. These symbols are notated immediately above the staff of the part that might be improvised—most often the piano part in a jazz, rock, or pop arrangement, but possibly a horn part for a featured solo or a vocal part for a featured scat solo. A published arrangement will usually also have a conventionally-notated part, to suggest the improvised style or to be read in case the performer is not a strong improvisor. In a style where improvisation is appropriate, the chord symbols allow the performer to infuse the part with some individuality or—in the case of the pianist who is not a strong reader—at least to provide a functional, harmonically-based accompaniment.

The most common chord symbols are realized in Example 2–7. Because the nomenclature is not yet standardized, two symbols are given for each sonority—the top one found in jazz music, the bottom one found in pop and show music.

What these symbols suggest to the improvisor is the essential chord quality. A folk or rock player might simply realize these symbols literally, while a jazz performer might add ninths, thirteenths, and the like as appropriate. These symbols also suggest the harmonic function of each chord, from which the improvisor generates melodic material.

Example 2–7. The most common chord symbols.

Jazz $C^\triangle$ Cmaj^7 C^7 C^{7}sus C-^{7} C-$^{7(b5)}$ C^{o7}
Pop C Cmaj^7 C^7 C^{7}sus Cm^7 C$^\emptyset$ C^{o7}

These symbols can also be used as an analytical shorthand, even when not noted in the music itself, and will be used along with Roman numerals to analyze harmonic structures throughout this book. Example 2–8 provides a quick review of chord symbols and Roman numeral functions for a progression in the key of F major. See Chapters 13 and 15 for a detailed discussion of these symbols.

Example 2–8. Harmonic analysis of a chord progression in F major.

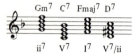

Stemming, Beaming, and Rests

When notes stand alone (i.e., are not beamed together), the stems go down if the note head is on or above the middle line and up if the head is below the middle line:

When notes are beamed together, stem direction depends on whether the majority of note heads are above or below the middle line:

When only two notes are involved, the note head farther from the middle line determines stem direction:

The purpose of the above principles is to keep most of the notation within the staff for easier reading.

Two notes a second apart which share the same stem are notated with the lower note on the left:

When each of these notes has its own stem, the stems must align vertically:

Notes of different rhythmic values may not share the same stem:

Fast notes should be beamed to indicate the beat:

"Half beats" may be linked as long as major subdivisions within the measure are maintained:

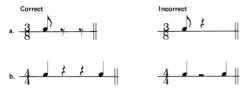

Rests should not be of greater value than the beat on which they begin in order to reflect the secondary stresses within the measure:

Each rest should be notated where it begins and should take up horizontal space on the staff corresponding to its value:

The one exception to this is the whole rest, which is centered in the measure and is used as a measure of rest for any meter signature:

Piano Notation

Piano notation can become rather complex, and the arranger is urged to study piano music or a book devoted to notation practice. However, the following points are illustrated in Example 2–9:

1. Notes sounding together must align vertically.

2. When one stem is shared by two or more pitches, note heads go to the left of the stem when the stem goes up, to the right when the stem goes down.

When note heads are a second apart, however, the lower one goes to the left and the upper one goes to the right of the stem. (See measure 4, treble clef, of Ex. 2–9.)

3. Different lines (rarely more than two) can be delineated on one staff by the use of different stem directions and rests. (See measure 1, treble clef.)

4. Arpeggios whose notes are to continue to ring can be written simply, with tie marks or pedal indications.

5. Pedal markings *Ped* ⌐ or *P* ⌐ may be used, ⌐⌐ indicating the release and then reapplication of the pedal. Unless otherwise indicated, pedal markings refer to the damper (''loud'') pedal, which acts to sustain the pitches played while the pedal is down. If a conventional piano style is used and pedal subtleties are not crucial, the arranger may write ''pedal freely'' and most pianists will respond appropriately.

Example 2–9. Piano notation.

For further discussion of writing for the keyboard, the reader is referred to Chapters 4 and 14.

Text Notation

In open and close score, the text generally goes below the staff of each vocal part. In close score, when all parts share the same text and essentially the same rhythm (as in an SATB hymn setting), the text goes between the two staves (Ex. 2–10).

Even with text, notes should be spaced within the measure so as to reflect their relative rhythmic values as much as possible. Words widely separated by a long note may be ''connected'' by a horizontal line (Ex. 2–11).
However, some allowance may have to be made so that the text can be written clearly and so that notes that sound together line up properly from part to part.

A word of more than one syllable is hyphenated according to dictionary usage (e.g., ''Child-ren nev-er eat their car-rots''), not necessarily as one might think it would be sung (e.g., ''Chil-dren ne-ver eat their ca-rrots'').

If one syllable is set to more than one note, those notes (called a *melisma* if there are more than a few) must be slurred together. A line (solid if short, broken

Example 2–10. Crüger (arr. J.S. Bach): *Schmücke dich, o liebe Seele*

Deck thy-self, my soul,— with glad - ness, Leave the
Come in - to the day - lights splen - dor, There with

gloom - y — haunts of sad - ness,
joy thy— prais - es ren - der

Example 2–11.

Correct

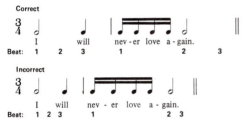

I will nev - er love a - gain.
Beat: 1 2 3 1 2 3

Incorrect

I will nev - er love a - gain.
Beat: 1 2 3 1 2 3

if it extends over more than one measure) may extend horizontally from the syllable to the last note value involved:

hel lo in there. _____

Observe, too, that punctuation (period, comma, question mark, exclamation point, etc.) *precedes* this horizontal line.

The old practice of further separating notes in a syllabic setting by giving each note its own flag is no longer used. The flags and beams should indicate metric groupings, while the slurs indicate how many notes are sung to each syllable:

If the arranger wishes to indicate where the singers are to breathe (particularly in a passage where there are no rests), a comma (,) or similar breath mark is placed above each staff at the point where the breath is to be taken. Should the arranger want to ensure that a breath *not* be taken—especially at a point such as a phrase ending where a singer might otherwise take a breath—dotted lines are used to "draw" the phrases together:

Text Declamation

Normal speech has its own rhythms, inflections, and accents. A composer will most often follow these aspects of the text being set, thereby enhancing and not obscuring its meaning. Because the arranger works to further enhance the text—manipulating the melody, harmony, rhythms, and textures, and creating counter-lines, figuration, and the like—he or she must be acutely aware of text declamation. It is recommended that the arranger speak each part aloud as it is written, using its rhythm and approximate pitch contour to see if the line sounds natural, that is, close to normal speech. The more natural the line, the easier to sing and to communicate, and, thus, the more convincing the performance.

Two basic principles will help to achieve this:

a. Stress important words in a phrase by means of higher pitch, syncopation, longer time value, thicker texture, and more chromatic harmony:

In the whole world, I love only *you*

b. Within a word, stress the syllable that receives stress in normal speech:

I *nev*-er ate a blue ca-*na*-ry

(Improper stress on the first syllable of canary makes the word sound like *can*nery, which changes the meaning of the phrase altogether.)

Even when the original source material is correct in its setting, the meaning can be greatly enhanced. Example 2–12 illustrates how, by altering only the rhythm, the line has more drive and sparkle because added stress is place upon the important words and pitches.

Example 2–12.

CHAPTER THREE

BASIC HARMONIC PRINCIPLES FOR CHORAL ARRANGING

THERE ARE A NUMBER OF WIDELY ACCEPTED HARMONIC PRINCIPLES that apply to all traditional music. The intent of this chapter is to focus on those principles that are most pertinent in choral arranging and to review them briefly rather than to present them in a comprehensive exposition of all harmonic practices. More detailed information on any of these topics can be found in any of the myriad of basic music theory texts currently on the market.

All the examples in this chapter will be presented in the context of the four-voice, SATB, note-against-note texture commonly found in hymn settings and many other traditional vocal forms. Although this four-voice texture is widely accepted as an ideal medium for presenting basic theoretical concepts, it needs to be understood that all these principles also apply to two-, three-, and other four-part textures, as well as to the accompaniments.

INITIAL HARMONIC CONCEPTS

These initial concepts concern the way in which the pitches of a single chord are placed on the staff.

Close and Open Voicing

Triads which are in *close position* have less than an octave between the upper three voices (soprano, alto, and tenor). Conversely, triads in *open position* have at least an octave between the soprano and tenor voices. Another way of stating this relationship is that in close position, no tone of the same triad can be inserted between soprano and alto, or between alto and tenor. Open position voicing allows tones to be inserted between these voices. In arranging, there needs to be a balance between close and open voicing as discussed in the section on note-against-note homophony in Chapter 10, and also illustrated in the mixed voicing example below.

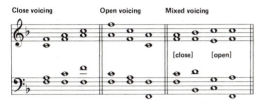

Chord Spacing

To avoid gaps, it is generally understood that there should be no more than an octave between soprano and alto, or alto and tenor, while there can be a distance greater than an octave between tenor and bass due to the latter's resonant qualities.

In the problematic spacings illustrated below, the choral voicings accentuate the following imbalances:

Chord A The soprano's sound is separate from the rest of the chorus;

Chord B The gap between men's and women's voices is heard;

Chord C The gap between men's and women's voices is accentuated, with the women in a bright register and the men in a register that projects less forcefully.

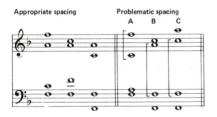

Inversion

Harmonic structures which have the root in the bass are in *root position*. When the third is located in the bass, the chord is in *first inversion*; when the fifth is in the bass, the chord is in *second inversion*. Harmonic progressions normally include both root position and inverted chords for variety, although root position chords predominate because they are more stable. Second inversion chords are particularly unstable and should not be overused; careful attention must be paid to their chords of approach and resolution.

Doubling

Since triads have only three unique pitches, in an SATB voicing it is necessary to double one of these pitches. The following is a general guideline for triad doubling, taking into account the harmonic factors of functional relationship and inversion.

1. Root position chords (with the exception of the vii° chord) double the root.

2. First inversion triads generally double the tonal degree (that member of the triad which is either the tonic, subdominant, or dominant pitch of the key). There is some freedom in applying this guideline, depending on voice leading or spacing considerations.

3. Second inversion triads always double the bass note (the fifth of the triad). It must be stressed here that second inversion $\binom{6}{4}$ chords are very restricted in their usage and appear infrequently, in either a passing or cadential application.

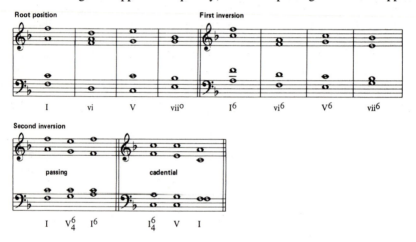

CHORD MOTION

Voice Leading and Tendency Tones

Good voice leading is a matter of common sense with a view toward making a single vocal line as singable as possible. To achieve this end, step motion usually predominates, while wide skips are used less frequently and an attempt is made to follow a wide skip with a step in the opposite direction wherever possible. When common tones exist between two adjacent chords, the common tone should be retained in the same voice part.

Certain pitches or intervals suggest a particular kind of voice leading or resolution based on their context. One of these is the seventh scale degree, or *leading tone*. Because of the strong tendency of the leading tone to move to the tonic, wherever possible the leading tone chord member should lead to the tonic in the following chord. Similarly, when a seventh chord (especially a major-minor seventh chord) is employed, the chord member which is the seventh has a strong tendency to resolve downward in the following chord.

Augmented and diminished intervals can be difficult to sing. In particular, the augmented second and augmented fourth ascending and the diminished fifth descending need to be approached and resolved carefully. Generally, the augmented intervals resolve outward, while diminished intervals resolve inward and thus involve a change in melodic direction.

Several of these voice-leading features can be observed in Example 3–1. Note the basic conjunct character of the upper three parts, with common tone retention (see for example, the alto part, measures 1–2). The bass line usually has the most skips because of movement from one chord root to another a fourth or fifth away (measures 1–3). The majority of the *e*♮ leading tones resolve to the tonic. The *e*♮ in the next-to-last chord resolves downward to the fifth scale degree in the tonic chord; otherwise, this tonic chord would omit the fifth and triple the root, which is still an acceptable procedure. The seventh in this next-to-last chord resolves downward.

Example 3–1. Traditional: *Coventry Carol*

In Example 3–2 below, the final four measures of Example 3–1 are rewritten to include an augmented second in the second measure of the alto part. This is not an easy interval to sing and should be avoided by either following the voice leading in Example 3–1 or resolving the alto *d*♭ to *c* and the tenor *f* to *e*.

Example 3–2. Traditional: *Coventry Carol*

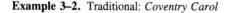

Parallel and Contrary Motion

When moving from one chord to another in conventional styles, contrary motion should be used as frequently as possible to achieve voice independence and an overall sense of balance. The last four measures of Example 3–1 provide a superlative example of this technique, where contrary motion is used in the outer voices to connect almost every chord in the passage. Similar motion may be necessary at times in particular chord progressions. The first measure of Example 3–1 presents an excellent illustration of this technique.

Parallel fifths or octaves work to the detriment of voice independence and should be avoided in conventional part-writing. In certain jazz and popular styles, such parallelism is appropriate where the voicings essentially serve to enhance the melodic line. Other intervals (thirds, sixths, and sometimes fourths) appear with some frequency as parallel intervals and do not cause the same concern.

Voice Crossing

There are occasions when it is necessary to cross voice parts because of voice leading or simply to add interest to a line. This is done primarily between the alto and tenor parts, which have the tendency to become static. Voice crossing between the soprano and alto is not recommended because of the possibility that the melodic line might be obscured. Likewise, the tenor and bass are not usually crossed, to keep the chord fundamental clearly sounding in the bass part.

Sometimes an arranger consciously chooses to cross the alto and tenor parts to bring particular intensity to one of the pitches in a chord by placing it in the higher tessitura of the tenor, where it will be emphasized. For instance, in measures 3 and 4 of Example 3–1, the tenors and altos could be crossed and still remain within range. This would tend to give weight to the resulting $db–c$ motion in the alto part. Normally, such voice crossing is not necessary, and the arranger should have a substantial musical reason for considering it.

CHORD VOCABULARY AND CHORD PROGRESSION IN MELODY HARMONIZATION

The choral arranger uses a pre-existent melody as the basis for a choral arrangement. Often the musical source for the choral arrangement may only be available in the form of a single-line melody with text. Before any real consideration of texture or accompaniment, the first step is to work out a basic harmonization for the melody.

Many melodies can be fully harmonized using only basic triads. Most of this section focuses on how to form logical musical progressions from these basic triads in the process of harmonizing a source melody. In addition, some consideration will be given to diatonic seventh chords and chromatic chords as agents of additional harmonic color.

Basic Triadic Harmony

The basic harmonic system is organized by the concept of *key*, where triads are built on each scale degree of the key using only pitches from the scale. Note the following triads which occur in the key of F major.

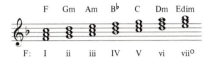

The key (capital letter for major, small letter for minor) appears below the key signature. Two chord designations are given above and below the triads. The top one shows the triad root and the quality: major (no designation), minor (m), diminished (dim), or augmented (aug). The Roman numeral shows the position of the chord within the key, with large numerals for major and small numerals for minor.

The same basic triads can be built in minor, as exemplified by the f minor scale with triads below.

The basic minor scale on which triads are built is *natural minor*. But frequently, the seventh scale degree is altered (as in *harmonic minor*), creating a leading tone. Hence, the chord built on the *dominant* (fifth scale degree) in minor can be either a minor (v) or a major (V) triad. Likewise, the triad occurring on the seventh degree is either major (VII) and built on the subtonic, or diminished (vii°) and built on the leading tone.

The most important and frequently emphasized triads in a key are the tonic (I), subdominant (IV), and dominant (V). Many songs can be harmonized using only these three triads; and when this occurs, the most frequent directional pattern is subdominant to dominant to tonic.

Since these three triads occur as the cornerstones of much traditional music, they are frequently called the three *primary* triads. The *secondary* triads relate functionally to the primary triads based partially on the number of common tones these triads share with the three primary triads. The iii and vi chords each share two tones with the tonic (I) chord and therefore frequently follow or substitute for it. The ii chord acts as a pre-dominant, like the subdominant (IV) chord with which it shares two tones. The vii° triad, a dominant like the V chord, is used less frequently than the other secondary triads.

In planning a progression, any secondary or primary triad can move directly to the tonic, but, in general, will tend to move in the predictable way from tonic (or the iii and vi substitutes), to subdominant (including the ii chord), to dominant, and finally back to tonic. This motion is graphically presented in the diagram below and can be seen in the context of Example 3–3 in the following section of the text.

TONIC	SUBDOMINANT	DOMINANT	TONIC
I(vi,iii)	IV(ii)	V(vii)	I

Melody Harmonization

The starting point for any choral arrangement is always the source melody. All the foregoing harmonic description must now be related to the source melody to see how certain aspects of melodic construction will affect the harmony. Consider the following as a general approach to harmonizing any source melody.

1. Decide on the key of the source melody.

2. Familiarize yourself with the chord members of all the primary and secondary triads in that key, initially concentrating on the primary triads (I, IV, V).

3. Decide which notes of the melody you will harmonize. Normally, notes that occur on accented beats have longer durations or repeat, and those that begin and end melodies are harmonized. Factors like tempo and meter also affect which notes are harmonized. For instance, in slow tempos all notes may be harmonized, as in a hymn tune. In faster tempos, some melody notes may be considered nonharmonic tones (passing tones, neighbor tones, etc.) and will not be harmonized.

4. Begin with the primary triads and match the melody note to be harmonized with the chord members of the primary triads. Remember that many melodies begin and end on the tonic and that chords move in a predictable direction as discussed in the previous section of this chapter. Write the chord symbol above and/or the Roman numeral below the melody note to be harmonized. If more than one primary triad fits the melody note, write both options.

5. Sing through the melody while playing the proposed primary triads or triad options on the piano and let your ear judge which chords fit the best.

6. Some melodies are constructed in such a way that a harmonization sounds complete and musically satisfying using only primary triads. However, most melody harmonizations are enhanced by adding secondary triads. Consider secondary triad harmonic substitutes where melody notes repeat and at other places in the melody where your ear tells you variety is needed, again following the general outline for harmonic motion presented earlier.

7. If the arrangement is for SATB, you may actually want to arrange a four-part, note-against-note setting using the selected triads. Otherwise, you may want to move forward to the next logical step in the arrangement as described in Chapter 8.

Example 3–3 illustrates a harmonization of *Good Christian Men, Rejoice* using only primary triads. All the melody notes are harmonized, although sometimes triads are repeated with changed voicings. Note that the eighth notes in measures 4–6 could also have been considered nonharmonic tones (neighbor tones and passing tones) and, consequently, not harmonized. Such a decision is based on the musical wishes of the arranger—here, a desire for faster harmonic rhythm—rather than on any definite right or wrong decision. Consider also how frequently the triads move in the predictable subdominant-dominant-tonic direction.

Example 3–3. Traditional: *Good Christian Men, Rejoice*

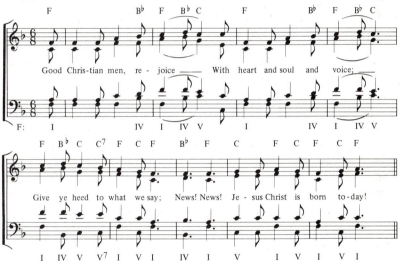

Example 3–4 is a logical extension of Example 3–3, where a number of secondary triads are added for harmonic variety and general musical interest. Notice particularly the use of the iii and vi chords in measures 3, 5, 6, and 9, as well as the ii chord (which usually occurs in first inversion) in measure 8. Other factors which make this a more balanced setting are the use of inverted primary triads (I^6 and I_4^6) and the change to open voicing in measures 4 and 5.

Diatonic Seventh Chords

The diatonic triad vocabulary can be extended by adding onto each scale degree triad a chord seventh. The diatonic seventh chords which result are described by two letters representing the type of triad (first letter) and the size of the interval of

Example 3–4. Traditional: *Good Christian Men, Rejoice*

the seventh (the second letter). The five different seventh chord sonorities are *major-major* (MM), *major-minor* (Mm), *minor-minor* (mm), *half-diminished* ($\emptyset$7), and *diminished* (o7). The half-diminished is sometimes referred to as *diminished-minor* and the diminished as a *fully diminished* seventh chord. The following chart shows these diatonic sevenths in the key of F major and f minor. It is useful to compare these with the chart of diatonic triads found earlier in the chapter. The sonorities shown for f minor do not include every possible seventh chord that can be constructed with various types of sixth and seventh scale degrees, but rather illustrate the most common types.

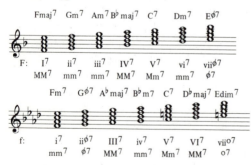

Although these seventh chords can freely substitute for their triadic equivalents to add color and spice to a harmonic setting, in practice they are used infrequently in traditional choral arrangements. They are particularly effective in slower moving passages where harmonic richness is desired. Particular mention should be made of the V7 chord, which is found in abundance in all styles of traditional music where it replaces the V chord, particularly at cadences.

The following setting of *Coventry Carol* contains many diatonic sevenths. Compare it carefully to Example 3–1, which uses only one seventh chord. Some of the seventh chords in Example 3–5 are substitute functions for the triads in Example 3–1, while others simply add the diatonic seventh to the triad. This arrangement of *Coventry Carol* has more diatonic sevenths than one might expect, to illustrate fully the harmonic potential of these sonorities. Often the diatonic seventh chord is used more sparingly to add color to a special musical moment.

Example 3–5. Traditional: *Coventry Carol*

Secondary Dominant Seventh Chords

One of the most common types of chromatic chords found in choral arrangements is the *secondary dominant* triad or seventh chord. The principle underlying the secondary dominant is that any major or minor diatonic triad in a key may be preceded by its dominant. In major, this means the dominant of I, ii, iii, IV, V, and vi, and in minor, of i, III, iv, V, VI, and VII. The symbol for the secondary dominant seventh is $V^7/$ (triad function). Since the secondary dominant seventh essentially transfers the V^7–I relationship to other diatonic triads, it follows that some notes of the seventh chord may require chromatics to make it a Mm^7 like the V^7. Also like the V^7 chord, the secondary dominant seventh chord can be used in all inversions and follows the established resolutions for the V^7 chord. Below find selected examples of secondary dominant seventh chords with resolutions in F major.

To incorporate secondary dominants into melody harmonization requires a little special consideration. The easiest place to accommodate them is at a cadence point,

Example 3–6. Traditional: *Good Christian Men, Rejoice*

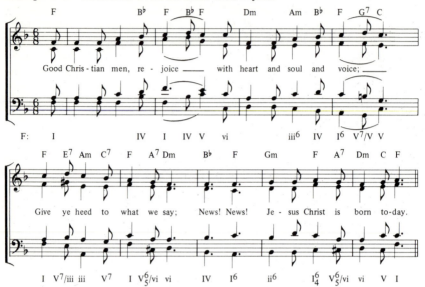

where a secondary dominant precedes the cadence chord. Theoretically, any triad can be preceded by its secondary dominant, but the melodic approach note to such a triad must be a member of the secondary dominant, and the addition of the secondary dominant must make musical sense.

Several secondary dominants have been added to the setting of *Good Christian Men, Rejoice* of Example 3–4 to create the setting found in Example 3–6. The cadence points in measures 4 and 6 are obvious places for secondary dominant embellishment. The inverted secondary dominant is chosen for measure 8 because of the obvious voice leading connection in the bass part.

Other Chromatic Chords

Aside from secondary dominants, the traditional chromatic vocabulary includes *embellishing diminished seventh* chords, the *Neapolitan sixth* chord, and *augmented sixth* chords. Since these last three chromatic types are used less frequently than secondary dominants in traditional choral arrangements, the reader is referred to a basic harmony text for explanations.

ARRANGING EXERCISES

In the exercises below, use an SATB note-against-note texture similar to the one occurring in the examples already cited in this chapter. Use good doubling and other voice-leading procedures.

1. Harmonize the folk song *I Know Where I'm Going*. Begin by using only primary triads, then add secondary triads. Try to use each secondary triad at least once.

2. Harmonize the folk song *Johnny Has Gone for a Soldier*. In the first version, use only primary triads. In a subsequent version, use several diatonic seventh chords.

3. Harmonize the spiritual *Were You There*, using primary and secondary triads. Add several secondary dominant seventh chords to include V^7 /IV, V^7 /V, and V^7 /vi.

CHAPTER FOUR

THE KEYBOARD ACCOMPANIMENT

EACH CHORAL ARRANGEMENT PRESENTS ITS OWN MUSICAL and technical challenges in the writing of the accompaniment. This chapter will be devoted to the role of the accompaniment, technical concerns in writing for piano and organ (the instruments most commonly used in accompanying), and certain styles of accompaniment. For a discussion of arranging for chorus with small instrumental ensembles, the reader is referred to Chapter 16.

THE ROLE OF THE ACCOMPANIMENT

The role of the accompaniment is primarily to:

1. Enhance the mood of the text and reinforce the style as projected by the vocal setting.

2. Provide tonal centers and harmonic structure, metric pulse and rhythmic impetus, and interest through counterpoint and embellishment.

3. Aid singers by providing pitches which anticipate vocal entrances, doublings of difficult vocal leaps and chromatic passages, and reinforcement of rhythmically difficult vocal figures.

4. Provide contrast to vocal sections through instrumental introductions, interludes, and endings.

5. Prepare the audience for a sudden change of mood.

6. ''Fill'' the space while the voices rest.

7. Contribute to the energy level and growth of the arrangement.

8. Unify the arrangement.

9. Be silent (or extremely thin and quiet) when the poignancy, pathos, humor, smoothness, or excitement of an unaccompanied passage is more effective.

1. Enhance the Mood of the Text and Reinforce the Style as Projected by the Vocal Setting

The text's mood may be enhanced through the dynamics, register, texture, rhythm, and counter-material of the accompaniment. In fact, the mood may be *generated* by the accompaniment (thus influencing the listener's perception of the text), as demonstrated by the three different accompaniments provided for the same melody in Example 4–1.

Example 4–1. *America* excerpt with three contrasting accompaniments.

Choral arrangements may be divided roughly into three basic stylistic categories—secular/traditional, sacred, and jazz/pop/rock—in that, as usually defined, they have emerged from distinct cultural traditions.

a. The secular/traditional styles range from ballads to marches to drinking songs. A successful accompaniment may create the appropriate environment by simulating the instruments originally associated with the genre: for example, guitar strumming with the ballad, fifes and drum rhythms with the march, and the oom-pah-pah of the German tavern band. The variations on this idea are limitless. For example, how raucous should the tavern band be? How many ''wrong'' notes might it play? Are the words very important, as in the telling of a story (subdued accompaniment), or are they repetitive, designed mainly for having a good time (active accompaniment with much variation)?

Because this music is based upon European and American folk traditions, accompaniments should be essentially triadic, metrically clear, and rhythmically repetitive—in a word, simple. Example 4–2 illustrates slight variety, clear phrase delineation, and support for the vocal lines—all within the very simple style of the tune.

b. Sacred arrangements project the emotional spectrum from the meditative to the joyous. With their roots in Western European religious and art music, sacred styles, too, are essentially triadic and metrically clear, but greater complexity is sometimes achieved through frequent use of nonharmonic tones such as passing, neighbor, and pedal tones, and suspensions. These nonharmonic tones are used in the accompaniment to color rather simple vocal parts or to

Example 4–2. Tom Paxton (arr. D. Riley and D. Wilson): *My Dog's Bigger Than Your Dog*

© 1982 Reprinted by permission of Cherry Lane Music Co.

Example 4–3. Hudson: *My Soul Doth Magnify the Lord*

lend support to the linear counterpoint of the vocal parts themselves (Ex. 4–3).

c. Contemporary jazz, rock, and pop styles synthesize European and African music in varying degrees. The three styles rely on a steady pulse against which frequently syncopated lines and chords sound. The harmonic material covers the spectrum from the triads predominating in much rock to the thirteenth chords with chromatic alterations of progressive jazz. Melodic material may be generated from conventional (major, minor, or modal) scales or from the blues scale. Because of the range and diversity of styles that must be considered in these idioms, Chapter 15 is devoted exclusively to the nature of their accompaniments.

2. Provide Tonal Centers and Harmonic Structure; Metric Pulse and Rhythmic Impetus; Interest Through Counterpoint and Embellishment

Example 4–4 illustrates how some of these concerns can be dealt with quite simply. All five chords cited serve to define the key of *B♭*. The pitches of the accompaniment are limited to chord tones, thus clarifying the harmonic structure and progression while at the same time providing good voice leading. (Note, for

Example 4–4. D. Besig: *Come Follow Me*

example, that the first notes of each chord to sound form a descending line: *Bb-A-G-F-Eb*.)

By beginning the accompaniment's ascending pattern on the downbeat, the meter is defined. The persistent eighth-note figure helps to define the meter and provide the gentle momentum called for by the text. Counterpoint and embellishment will be focused upon later in this chapter, in the discussion of style.

As a rule of thumb, the less these elements are present in the vocal writing, the more they must be present in the accompaniment. A unison vocal line will usually require an accompaniment that fills out the harmony; a vocal line of half notes will require notes of shorter duration in the accompaniment. In this way a balance is achieved for the listener.

3. Provide Tonal and Rhythmic Support for the Singers

One of the greatest dangers an arranger faces is in expecting too much from a choir. Unlike the writer who is working in solitude, often with the aid of a piano, the singer is performing amid twelve to one hundred other signers, most of whom may be singing other material, and none of whom can reach out to an instrument for periodic pitch confirmation. Therefore the arranger must anticipate challenges to the singers and support them in the following ways—keeping in mind that the younger or less experienced the singers, the more such support is necessary.

a. Prepare vocal entrances by first giving their pitches in the accompaniment (preferably in the same register), or by making their entrance pitch "inevitable," as shown in Example 4–5. Here the anticipation of the unison *ab* is made possible by the scalar run in the accompaniment, even though a modulation is also taking place.

Example 4–5. Traditional (arr. W. Barker): *Patriotic Pageantry*

stuck a feath-er in his cap and called it mac-a-ro - ni.

stuck a feath-er in his cap and called it mac-a-ro - ni.

Hear the flutes!

Hear the flutes!

b. Double awkward leaps or extensive chromatic passages in inner voices where the lines may be difficult to pre-hear, or in the melody or bass for the sake of choral intonation. Of course, the accompaniment must also have its own linear and harmonic logic, so this voice doubling should be made part of the ongoing accompanimental texture. In Example 4–6, the right-hand part of the accompaniment reinforces the soprano leap and then confirms the harmonies while supporting the vocal syncopation and capturing the overall style of the passage. Such support would be essential for, say, the average high school chorus.

4. Provide Contrasting Sections

Keyboard accompaniments may provide introductions, interludes, and endings to establish or change mood, key center, tempo, meter, or style. Of course, the

Example 4–6. Riley and Wilson: *Love Is Movin' My Way*

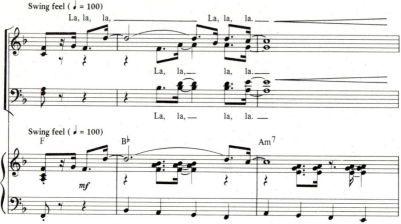

chorus may be involved in these changes as well, but the role of the accompaniment here is usually crucial. Furthermore, the timbral contrast provided by the solo piano or organ contributes a new (and often much needed) dimension to an arrangement. Generally, the longer and more involved the arrangement, the more such sections are appropriate. The reader is referred to Chapters 7 and 8 for technical and aesthetic concerns in writing these sections.

The accompaniment may help to delineate the arrangement's formal shape. The source melody itself may be either *strophic* (A, A^1, A^2, etc.), or *sectional* (such as *AABACA*). With strophic form, the accompaniment may group certain verses together, or interest and growth may be brought to the strophic tune by a slight (or dramatic) change in the accompaniment with each verse:

SOURCE FORM:	A	A^1	A^2	A^3	A^4	A^5
ACCOMPANIMENT'S MATERIAL:	W*	W	X	X	Y	Z

| | Two verses are linked. | Verses are separated from one another, and each accompanimental texture now lasts for only one verse, providing a sense of acceleration to the arrangement. |

---

*W might be chordal, X chordal with faster rhythms, Y arpeggios, Z arpeggios with countermelody, etc.

The sectional nature of other source melodies may be emphasized by a corresponding sectionalization of the accompaniment or de-emphasized by little change in the accompaniment from one section to the next:

SOURCE FORM:	A	A^1	B	A^1	C	A^2
ACCOMPANIMENT'S MATERIAL:	X	X^1	X^1	X^1	Y	Y^1

Here the accompaniment tends to connect the A, A^1, B, and A^1 sections, while helping to focus upon the contrasting nature of the C section. The final A^2 returns essentially to the source melody's opening material but is linked to C through the accompanimental texture or style.

5. Create a Sudden Change

A single gesture or several measures in the accompaniment can prepare the audience for a change of key, tempo, mood, or style. This must be done only if the text warrants it and if the arrangement's pacing is well served. The two-part arrangement of *Sing a Rainbow* is in the form:

A B A^1 Interlude A B^1 A^2

While most of the arrangement employs an accompaniment that is high in register or lyrical in nature or both, the interlude and following A section employ a low, repetitive accompanimental figure (excerpted in Example 4–7) for contrast. The interlude beginning in measure 4 of the example, serves to create the new mood and break up the eight-bar phrasing of each section of the source melody.

6. Fill the Space

Singers need to breathe and the audience needs to breathe psychologically along with the singers, but usually the energy level must be maintained. To allow for both, the accompaniment must fill the space between vocal phrases and lead the singers and audience into the next phrase. The fill provides contrast but must be appropriate to the passage. Example 4–8 illustrates this device in two very different styles.

7. Contribute to the Energy Level and Growth of the Arrangement

Most arrangements move from the simple to the more complex in order to keep the listener involved. Certain elements that contribute to growth—extended range, change of register, faster rhythms (♩ ♩ → ♫ ♫ → ♬ ♬), number of pitches sounding at once—can be most easily executed in the accompaniment. Example 4–9 exhibits very common accompanimental patterns, found here on *one* arrangement. Note that such dramatic changes also contribute to the formal design of the arrangement.

Example 4–7. Hamilton (arr. J. Coates): *Sing a Rainbow*

Example 4–8a. Spence, Keith, and Bergman (arr. D. Riley and D. Wilson): *Nice 'n' Easy*

Example 4–8b. Hamilton (arr. J.Coates): *Sing a Rainbow*

Example 4–9. Miller and Jackson (arr. H. Ades): *Let There Be Peace on Earth*

a. At rehearsal letter A.

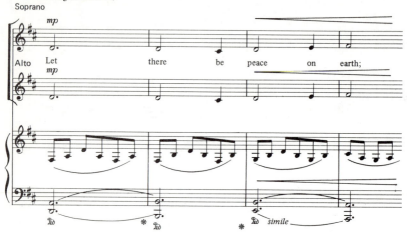

b. At rehearsal letter F.

c. Last ten bars.

And   let   it   be - gin —— with   me,

with ——   me! ——

Note the depth and power with which the piece ends, even though it is only a two-part (SA) setting. The voices provide the high, bright sonorities while the accompaniment provides the rest. Note also that, despite the density of the piano chords, the accompaniment as well the vocal parts are technically easy to execute.

Often choral material is simple and repetitive, in part so that it can be learned quickly. The burden of creating variation and interest, then, falls on the accompaniment and may be expressed through more dense sonorities, wider range, different registers or increased counterpoint, with the degree of subtlety being determined by the passage. Example 4–10 involves a return of the opening vocal material (for children's chorus), but the accompaniment provides new interest, while maintaining

Example 4–10. Wilson (text by R. L. Stevenson): *My Shadow*

quiet simplicity, and projects the fact that the child's shadow is still asleep, by quoting Brahms' *Lullaby* within the arrangement's $\frac{4}{4}$ meter.

8. Unify the Arrangement

The accompaniment can serve to unify the arrangement through such techniques as the following:

a. Repetition of a distinctive melodic or rhythmic pattern that is a major motive of the tune.

b. Repetition, particularly of a rhythmic motive, that is suggestive of a specific style—as the bolero rhythm in the accompaniment to the song *Man of La Mancha* serves to unify, as well as to conjure up Moorish exoticism.

c. Expanding upon an accompanimental figure so that, for example, the material that once provided a quiet, flowing undercurrent (Ex. 4–11a) evolves into a dramatic gesture (Ex. 4–11b).

Example 4–11.

a. Original, quiet and flowing sixteenth-note accompaniment.

b. The pattern as a dramatic gesture.

9. Be Silent When Necessary

Sometimes the drama of the moment is best served by silence in the accompaniment—for a brief moment of total silence or for an *a cappella* passage. This can be either abrupt, to capture the declamatory nature of the text (Ex. 4–12a), or smooth, to contribute to the floating nature of an *a cappella* phrase (Ex. 4–12b). Above all, the unaccompanied vocal lines which result must be easy to sing.

Example 4–12a. Traditional (arr. M. Wilson and W. Ehret): *Throw It Out the Window*

Harry Wilson and Walter Ehret, *Prentice-Hall Choral Series,*
Book 5, Englewood Cliffs, NJ, 1961. Reprinted by permission.

Note that in both of these examples, this dramatic change in texture is reserved for near the end of the arrangement.

TECHNICAL CONSIDERATIONS

The keyboard accompaniment for an elementary or middle school-level arrangement should be particularly easy to play, not only to give straightforward support to the young voices but also because the music teacher usually conducts and accompanies simultaneously. The accompanist for high school and college groups usually comes from among the student ranks, and the level of difficulty should be geared accordingly. The church choir director is often also the accompanist, but here keyboard ability may be substantial.

Example 4–12b. Spence, Keith, and Bergman (arr. D.Riley and D. Wilson): *Nice 'n' Easy*

Conventional bass parts of the accompaniment should stay within the two octaves below middle C(c^1). For most of the arrangement, the right-hand part should stay within the one-and-one-half octaves above middle C, as it is in this register of the piano (and of the organ with conventional registrations) that "body" is achieved from chords, while at the same time, voice leading remains clear. The right hand may venture below or above this register, of course, for dramatic effect or temporary change of color or weight.

The top line of the accompaniment may sound in the register lower than, higher than, or the same as that of the highest vocal part. It may double the part at the unison or octave, or it may play counter-material. The lowest part of the accompaniment, however, should stay at the same pitch as, or lower than, the lowest vocal part, so that the vocal part does not at times protrude unsupported. (The exception, of course, is when the accompaniment clearly provides only nonreinforcing material such as a high trill or arpeggio.)

There are only a few technical differences between the piano and organ that must be considered in writing a conventional accompaniment. Piano sonorities begin to decay immediately after the keys are depressed, but the pitches can be sustained somewhat after the fingers have left the keys by means of the damper pedal. This means that more than ten pitches can be ringing at one time, but the keys must be periodically restruck if the pitch is to continue to sound. The reverse is true with the organ: the sonority stops as soon as the finger is lifted from the key, but as long as the key remains depressed, its pitch will continue to sound at a consistent volume. Also unlike the piano, most organs have pitched foot pedals to add another voice of striking depth, swell boxes to increase or decrease the volume gradually, and varied registration to alter the tone color and register of the pitches. Unless the arranger is very familiar with the instrument, it is best to write a conventional two-stave organ accompaniment, leaving appropriate pedaling and registration to the performer.

STYLES OF ACCOMPANIMENT

The arranger should be aware of certain basic styles of accompaniment, best categorized in terms of *choral doubling, arpeggiation, counter-material, rhythm, sustaining,* and *special effects.* Naturally, a given arrangement may call upon various styles from section to section. The reader is reminded that a discussion of jazz, rock, and pop styles of accompaniment can be found in Chapter 15.

Choral Doubling

Clearly, exact doubling of the vocal parts, the least independent of accompanimental styles, is used when such ''block'' writing is desired for support and enhancement of the choral texture, as in conventional hymn settings. This homophony often provides a sense of direct simplicity.

In certain settings where more weight must be given to the melodic line, the accompaniment may double that part, taking care to include other notes as well to enhance the melodic flow (Ex. 4–13).

Arpeggiation

In order to express clearly a passage's harmonic structure while providing a certain flowing momentum, the chord may be arpeggiated—often in the right-hand part, with simpler left-hand support (see Examples 4–4 and 4–9). The lower in register the accompanimental pattern, the wider the distance between pitches, to compensate for the thicker sound of each note. Also, as mentioned earlier, good voice leading is often maintained from at least the top note of one arpeggiated chord to that of the next.

Rhythmic Patterns and Figures

Many styles of music are expressed immediately through their rhythmic patterns. In such cases, accompaniments can serve to capture such styles through clear reiteration of those rhythmic patterns.

Marches and up-tempo folk songs and show tunes in $\frac{4}{4}$ meter rely upon the chord root and fifth in the bass *on* the beat, ''answered'' by a right-hand triad in

Example 4–13. Shire and A. & M. Bergman (arr. J. Nowak): *The Promise*

Theme from the Universal Picture "THE PROMISE" (I'll Never Say "Good-bye"). Words by Alan & Marilyn Bergman. Music by David Shire. © 1978, 1979 by LEEDS MUSIC CORP, DUCHESS MUSIC CORP. Rights administered by MCA MUSIC, A Division of MCA INC., New York. Used by permission, all rights reserved.

the keyboard's middle register on the *offbeat*.[1] To avoid monotony, this pattern should be broken at cadence points and the like by interjecting stepwise eighth notes in the bass or faster "fills" in the right-hand part. However, it is the simplicity and vital pulse that are infectious in the march, for example, and they must be the primary contribution of the accompaniment (Ex. 4–14).

---

[1]Often the notation of this pattern is augmented, placing the root and fifth on the first and third beats, respectively, and the right-hand chord on beats 2 and 4.

Example 4–14. Traditional (arr. G. Grier and L. Everson): *Dancing with Uncle Sam*

© 1980 The Heritage Music Press. Reprinted with permission.

The slow waltz has a clearly defined rhythmic pattern in $\frac{3}{4}$ meter, with the root and fifth alternating on the downbeats, and the right hand playing chords on beats 2 and 3. Note in Example 4–15, that the several voices are doubled in the accompaniment, while the rhythmic pattern of the waltz is maintained.

A faster waltz is the same, except that often the right hand plays only a half-note chord on beat 2.

Sometimes a rhythmic pattern combines with arpeggiation to form a rhythmic figure which provides momentum, unity, and interest. Example 4–16 employs essentially two accompanimental patterns: that found in measure 1 and repeated in measure 2, and the dotted pattern of measures 3–5. The pattern in measures 6–8 is a variation of the first pattern. The patterns are very conventional, but the

Example 4–15. Rice, Brown, and Daniels (arr. H. Wilson and W. Ehret): *You Tell Me Your Dream*

Harry Wilson and Walter Ehret, *Prentice-Hall Choral Series,*
Book 3, Englewood Cliffs, NJ, 1961. Reprinted by permission.

symmetrical vocal phrases $(2+2+2+2$ measures) are kept fresh by the unconventional repetition $(2+3+3$ measures) of the accompaniment's rhythmic patterns. Most of the arrangement relies on these two patterns in various combination.

Still greater interest emerges when melodic embellishment becomes part of the repeated rhythmic figure. This works particularly well in a slow arrangement where the vocal phrases are short and the accompaniment must fill consistently at the end of one or two measures. A simple but effective example of this is found in Example 4–17, where the entire accompaniment is devoted to chord tones except on the fourth beat of each measure, where the right hand plays a passing tone. In measures 1 and 3, this passing tone reinforces a vocal line, while in measures 2 and 4, it serves to fill the space by creating brief tension.

Example 4–16. Artman: *I'm Okay and You're Okay*

Example 4–17. Wilson and Knox: *Sing Alleluia!*

Counter-Material

As the accompaniment's melodic material assumes its own linear direction, independent counter-material emerges. Particularly when the melodic contour is restricted in order to best project the action or deep meaning of the text, such counter-material is necessary to provide musical interest. In Example 4–18, this is achieved without overpowering the vocal writing.

Counter-material often serves to lead into the next vocal sub-phrase. Such is the case in Example 4-19, where the accompaniment echoes the vocal melody with a harmonically-supported counterline that is still clearly subservient to the vocal material.

Counter-material may assume a great deal of melodic independence as long as it does not distract from, or dominate, the choral writing. Most often it should remain outside the choral register (usually higher) and have contrasting shape and rhythm. This was illustrated in Example 4–10. In Example 4–19, the high, triadic countermelody contrasts with the middle-register, stepwise tune. When counter-material is a complete melody in itself, it is usually best to introduce either the vocal melody or the accompanimental counter-melody earlier in the arrangement, before they are heard together.

Unconventional Voicings

An unconventional harmonic approach to the accompaniment can provide a fresh context for a well-known and straightforward source melody. Reharmonization, adding diatonic sevenths and ninths to triads, putting chords in inversion where root position is expected, and building chords in fourths or fifths rather than thirds can provide this freshness without making unusual demands on the singers. In

Example 4–18. Ray: *Remember This*

Example 4–19. Van Heusen (arr. D. Riley and D. Wilson): *Darn That Dream*

Example 4–20. Traditional (arr. W. Barker): *Patriotic Pageantry*

Example 4–21, the source melody is sung in canon, while the accompaniment provides a beautiful, somewhat unconventional setting. The first chord of the introduction suggests a I chord (G major), yet the seventh of the chord is the lowest note and the third is missing; the fourth measure suggests a V^7 chord (D^7), but the leading tone $f\sharp$ never appears; when the voices enter in the fifth bar, the conventional I chord is replaced by a IV chord (C major) with a passing d^1 in the right hand; when D^7 is finally heard in the sixth bar, its resolution to G is interrupted by a rest.

Too much harmonic color and ambiguity can bring most unsatisfying results. In the artfully conceived arrangement whose introduction and partial A section are

Example 4–21. Traditional (arr. S. Adler): *How Sweet the Sound*

cited in Example 4–21, the strophic song is accompanied in the rest of the arrangement as follows:

A^1—More conventional progressions and voicings, counterbalanced by a running eighth-note countermelody;

Interlude—Accompaniment only, employing texture of the introduction, leading into a modulation up a major second;

A^2—*A cappella* (accompaniment silent);

Ending—Accompaniment only, employing texture of the introduction.

Special Effects

To capture the sound of drums, bagpipes, chimes, sleigh bells, birds, or thunder, arrangers often create special effects in the keyboard writing. The possibilities, limited only by the writer's imagination, can lend great freshness to an arrangement. But the arranger must be vigilant in making sure the effects integrate well into the arrangement as a whole (possibly returning later in the arrangement) and do not overpower the choral writing. One such effect, of sleigh bells, is shown in Example 4–22. In this arrangement, the special effect is used only in the introduction (to create an environment for the opening text "Bells are ringing" and the song as a whole) and the ending, serving to unify the arrangement. (Introductions and endings are discussed further in Chapter 7.)

Example 4–22. McGlohon (arr. w. Ehret): *It's Christmas Time*

Sometimes the absence of pulse is desirable in the accompaniment, whether by silence or by a sustained sonority. Sustaining a sonority in the accompaniment while the voices move can be particularly effective in introductions, endings, and recitative-type passages where the isolation of the text is important. Naturally, because of its sustaining ability, this device works well on the organ, whereas on the piano the sonorities have to be rearticulated periodically.

SUMMARY

The accompaniment's independence and difficulty are governed by the musical intent of the passage, the level and abilities of the chorus and accompanist, and the degree to which the singers must be supported in difficult passages. The arranger should take care *not* to write:

a. A series of unrelated melodic materials just for the sake of vocal reinforcement;

b. Harmonies that conflict with melodic pitches (for example, a C major triad in the accompaniment while the voice is still singing an *f* before resolving to the *e* of the chord);

c. A *series* of syncopated rhythms in the right-hand part against straight quarter notes in the left-hand part—syncopation in both hands often being easier to perform;

d. Technically awkward textures, such that if the non-pianist arranger cannot play them at least at half speed, they should probably not be written.

The sign of a successful accompaniment is that it functions according to what is required at the moment, while giving the impression that it has its own integrity without overpowering the chorus. Its role is to help the singers perform well, while at the same time contributing fundamentally to the arrangement's shape, quality, and effectiveness.

ARRANGING EXERCISES

1. Provide a simple piano accompaniment—essentially chordal with a repeated rhythmic pattern—for the following traditional tune, arranged for an elementary school chorus.

2. In the following sacred setting, provide an arpeggiated accompaniment that would be effective played on either piano or organ.

Oh ho - ly night, __ the stars were bright - ly shin - ing.

3. Provide a triumphant closing for the following march excerpt. As the setting is for men's chorus, be sure to compensate for the lower vocal registers with brilliant piano sonorities.

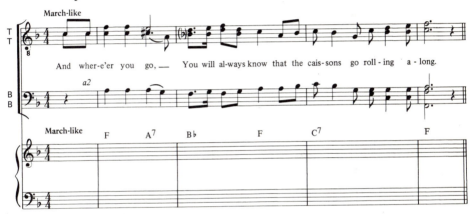

And wher-e'er you go, __ You will al-ways know that the cais-sons go roll - ing a - long.

4. Maintain the pulse, but support the vocal lines as necessary in the following setting for high school chorus. Brief silence is also possible.

Hol - di - ri - di - a, hol - di - ri - di - a, hol - di - ri - a,

(Continued next page)

CHAPTER FIVE

TWO-PART ARRANGING

THE TWO-PART ARRANGEMENT SERVES AS AN EXCELLENT starting point for choral arranging, since many of the homophonic and polyphonic textures and arranging principles used in two-part writing are expanded in three- and four-part writing. Arranging in polyphonic textures requires considerable skill which can most easily be gained through experience in writing for two voices.

Harmonic materials in two-part writing are quite restricted, since complete harmonies are not possible with only two voices. For this reason, most two-part arrangements are accompanied by keyboard, allowing the keyboard to fill out the harmony as well as provide additional rhythmic and melodic support for the setting.

TYPICAL VOICE COMBINATIONS

Most two-part arrangements are labelled *SA* or *two-part treble*. Many such arrangements are intended for the mature soprano and alto, but in practice many can also be sung by young children's voices in what is called the *equal-voice combination*. Some contemporary arrangers writing for young, unchanged voices label the arrangement *two-part* and on the score use Roman numerals I and II to indicate the equal-voice nature of the setting and also to avoid an all-female designation where unchanged voices are singing. Other two-voice combinations include SB or TB, usually occurring as small sections of larger SATB or TTBB pieces; the two-part arranging principles, however, are the same. The discussion in this chapter will focus on the SA or equal-voice combination.

HOMOPHONIC TEXTURES

Note-Against-Note

One of the most common textures found in two-part arranging is the note-against-note texture. Used with melodies that have fairly active rhythmic patterns, this texture adds a second voice, usually below the melody, using the same rhythmic values. The second part frequently parallels the original part in contour, primarily at the consonant intervals of a third or sixth. Less consonant intervals like the perfect fourth can be used sparingly if the added voice forms a chord tone against the original voice and the remaining chord members are filled in by the keyboard.

Example 5–1 illustrates a setting which is exclusively in note-against-note texture. Parallel thirds are the predominant interval choice between the parts, but

Example 5–1. Traditional (arr. H. Wilson and W. Ehret): *Spin, Spin, My Darling Daughter*

Harry Wilson and Walter Ehret, *Prentice-Hall Choral Series,*
Book 5, Englewood Cliffs, NJ, 1961. Reprinted by permission.

observe that the notes of the other intervals which appear in the second and seventh measures are both members of the primary harmony in the keyboard. From a musical standpoint this interval change is necessary to avoid the dullness of exclusive parallel third or sixth writing.

A similar approach is seen in Example 5–2. The voices move in parallel thirds and sixths, with occasional unisons and perfect fourths, chosen and voiced to reflect the "country" flavor of the tune. Observe that both Example 5–1 and Example 5–2 have melodies with fairly active rhythmic patterns.

Animated Homophony

This texture is an expansion of the note-against-note texture: the added voice, again usually written below the melody, embellishes the chord tones of the note-against-note texture with additional notes. This texture, not nearly as common as note-against-note, is often used to provide variation to an otherwise strict note-against-note treatment. The choral arranger is first advised to arrange a note-against-note texture, and then add the embellishing tones for the animated homophony.

Example 5–3 shows a mixture of note-against-note and an animated homophonic texture.

CONTRAPUNTAL TEXTURES

Countermelody

The most common way of creating contrapuntal texture in two-part arrangements is the *countermelody*. A countermelody is an independent line sounding against a given melody, maintaining separate pitch, rhythm, and contour, while remaining predominantly consonant with the original. Typically, a countermelody achieves independence primarily through rhythm. That is, a countermelody tends to complement the rhythm of the melody so that sustained notes are used against a rhythmically active portion and *vice versa*.

Countermelodies can be written above or below the original melody. Sometimes the parts cross; if a countermelody does cross the original melody, it will normally remain substantially above or below it to maintain the two-line independence.

A countermelody can be assigned either a text or a neutral vowel sound, depending on its rhythmic activity and its pitch relationship with the original melody. Such sounds as "oo" or "ah" (as described in Chapter 11) can be used when the original text and melody should be predominant, or when the dynamic level or character of the text suggests a more restrained countermelody. If a text is preferable, it is usually derived from or closely related to the text of the original, although a separate, unrelated text can be used to create tension leading to the climax of the arrangement.

Example 5–2. Connor (arr. D. Riley and D. Wilson): *Grandma's Feather Bed*

Example 5–3. Carey (arr. J. Coates, Jr.): *America*

Example 5–4 illustrates an active countermelody which both complements and duplicates the rhythm of the original melody. Note that the countermelody is consonant with the original, with chord tones predominating between the parts. The text is clearly derived from the original, although it does not sound simultaneously. Unity is achieved in the countermelody though repetition of a melodic motif.

Example 5–4. Coleman (arr. R. Barnes): *The Rhythm of Life*

The countermelody in Example 5–5 uses the neutral syllable "oo" and exemplifies a more sustained approach with longer rhythmic values. These musical features complement the more lyrical nature of the melody, contrasting with the driving rhythm of Example 5–4. The pitches of the countermelody are primarily consonant chord tones.

Example 5–5. Besig (words by Don Besig and Marcy Henchen, music by Don Besig): *A Better World*

Descant

Frequently, additional lines that are essentially countermelodies are labelled *descants*. Whereas countermelodies may appear above or below the original melody, descants are almost always written above the melody. The most consistent use of the term is in sacred hymn tunes, where the arranger provides an added upper line to the last verse of the hymn, typically to be performed by sopranos while other voices are singing the unison melody or the existing four parts of the hymn. One rhythmic approach to descant assigns primarily the same rhythmic values as the original melody, while another approach is based on the rhythmic freedom associated with the countermelody. From a harmonic standpoint, the descant is consonant with the melody, using almost exclusively chord tones with occasional embellishment.

Example 5–6 shows a descant which duplicates the rhythmic values of the *What Child Is This* melody. Although visually similar to the homophonic note-against-note texture, the descant, soaring above the melody, produces a remarkably different effect. Observe that it duplicates the melody for the first measure of each

Example 5–6. Traditional: *What Child Is This*

Example 5–7. Smart: *Angels, From the Realms of Glory*

phrase before beginning an independent melodic course, and also cadences on the same tonic note as the original. It should be noted that many descants cadence on the third or fifth of the tonic triad to bring the final verse to a triumphant close. Harmonically, the notes of this descant are all chord tones.

Most of the descant line in Example 5–7 also lies above the melody. In this approach there is rhythmic independence in the characteristic passing tone figures at the beginning of the descant, while rhythmic duplication exists in measures 2 and 3. Consonant chord tones predominate, with the descant cadencing on the fifth of the tonic triad against the tonic note of the melody.

Figuration

A *figuration* is a non-continuous, fragmentary added line that provides rhythmic and melodic punctuation to the original melody. This type of contrapuntal treatment is applied when the rhythm of the original melody tends to alternate between measures that are fairly active and those that are sustained. The figuration then enters at the point in the melody where there is little or no motion. Most figurations employ a text fragment that occurs in the melody immediately preceding the entrance of the figuration.

The first figuration in Example 5–8 is actually an imitation of the original melody. The figuration in measure 7 uses the neutral syllable "oo," while the last one utilizes a text fragment from the preceding measure. The melody actually appears here with a supporting voice below in strict parallel thirds or sixths. What still predominates is the melody with the figuration.

The figuration in Example 5–9, as that in Example 5–8, acts as a punctuation during the sustained part of the melody. In this case an original text fragment is used which relates to the text line immediately preceding it. This figuration appears initially in the second verse, and therefore helps to connect this verse with the homophonic presentation of the melody in the first verse. In both examples the non-continuous, fragmentary characteristics of figurations are evident.

Example 5–8. Miller and Jackson (arr. H. Ades): *Let There Be Peace on Earth*

(Continued next page)

Ostinato

An *ostinato* is a repeated motive that has rhythmic and pitch components. Typically one or two measures long, the choral ostinato reiterates a single text fragment related to or extracted from the original melody. Most ostinatos stay at one pitch level, although occasionally an ostinato will change pitch level after it has been established; thus the best melodies for ostinato treatment are those which imply the same harmony (usually tonic) for several measures. Often an ostinato is

Example 5–9. Paxton (arr. D. Riley and D. Wilson): *My Dog's Bigger Than Your Dog*

stated first without the melody to provide contrast in the arrangement and to establish it fully before it sounds against the melody.

In Example 5–10 the two-measure ostinato is stated alone before it continues below the melody. The melody in this example is well chosen for an ostinato treatment since it retains tonic harmony prominently throughout and has a strong forward-driving rhythm. The ostinato of the vocal part fits both the tonic in the melody and the mediant chords in the accompaniment.

Imitation

Imitation can be used as a choral arranging device to begin new sections of an arrangement or to set off a new line of text. Usually only one or at the most two measures of a melody are treated imitatively. Immediately after the imitation, the texture usually simplifies to some type of homophonic treatment. Typical pitch levels of imitation are the unison, octave, fifth, and fourth. Care must be taken to be sure that the harmonic implication of the original melody will fit the imitated voice during the time the imitation takes place.

Example 5–11 is typical of the use of imitation to set off a new section of text in the piece. Here the basic idea is two measures long and is imitated at the perfect fourth above. Observe that the two parts are treated homophonically when the imitation breaks off.

Canon

In a canonic texture, both vocal parts are assigned the same melody, although starting at different points and sometimes on different pitches. *Canon at the unison*, sometimes called a *round*, does not have the wide application that imitation has in

Example 5–10. Traditional (arr. R. Herrold): *Here Comes the Parade*

Example 5–11. Sitton: *Song of Praise*

choral arranging, because not all melodies have the musical properties that allow for an extended canonic treatment. Whereas imitation usually breaks off into a different texture after one or two measures in most choral arrangements, canon normally proceeds for a minimum of four measures and often up to eight measures or more. Canon at the unison or octave, sometimes called a *round*, is the most easily adopted for choral arrangements, and most canons start after one or two measures. Melodies that have a static tonic harmony throughout are the ones that work best for canon, and one of the first steps an arranger needs to take when examining a potential melody for arranging is to consider the melody for canonic possibilities. In some arrangements the canon will break off at the point where the static harmony makes a substantial change. Frequently if the harmonic change in the original melody (the leader of the canon) is slight, the second voice (the follower of the canon) may have a slight note variation to maintain a consonant intervallic relationship with the leader.

The canon in Example 5–12 is a unison canon with a two-measure separation. The arranger realized that *Yankee Doodle* was an excellent prospect for a canonic arrangement, because the tonic harmony remains static for six measures. In the seventh measure the dominant harmony appears and it is in this measure that the follower voice breaks off the canon, although the canon would normally break at this point for the cadence anyway. In this setting of *Yankee Doodle*, the immediate canonic treatment is justified because of the familiarity of the tune. In choral arrangements of melodies less well known than *Yankee Doodle*, a canonic treatment would best be reserved for the interior of the arrangement to allow the melody to become established in a simple setting first.

Example 5–12. Traditional (arr. R. Herrold): *Here Comes the Parade*

© 1975 Shawnee Press, Inc., Delaware Water Gap, PA 18327.
Used by permission.

Example 5–13. Traditional: *Ezekial Saw the Wheel* and *Now Let Me Fly*

Partner Songs

A highly specialized type of contrapuntal relationship exists where two pre-existent songs can be sung together simultaneously. This relationship, which is also known as *quodlibet*, is only possible if the harmony implied by the songs is identical and both are in the same key. The most effective partner songs are those which complement each other rhythmically and which avoid extensive unisons. Partner song relationships can be discovered by the arranger through extensive experimentation and knowledge of harmonic patterns in a wide variety of literature.

The spirituals *Ezekial Saw the Wheel* and *Now Let Me Fly*, as seen in Example 5–13, make effective partner songs. Not only are the rhythms complementary, but the different melodic contours and ranges also contribute to the independence of the two songs. Note also that each song has a subphrase cadence every two measures that is always on two different members of the same tonic triad.

MODEL ARRANGEMENTS

Sing a Rainbow (arr. J. Coates, Jr.)
Music contained in Appendix II.

The basic form for the song *Sing a Rainbow* is ABA, with each section eight measures long. The overall structure for the arrangement of this song is as follows:

ARRANGEMENT FORM	Intro	A	B	A'	Interlude	A"	B	A'''	Ending
TOTAL MEASURES	2	8	8	8	5	8	8	8	7
REHEARSAL LETTERS IN SCORE		A	B	C	D	E	F	G	H

Many of the textures discussed in this chapter exist in this arrangement as can be observed in the following:

Rehearsal A: Unison (4 measures), note-against-note (4 measures)
Rehearsal B: Countermelody
Rehearsal C: Imitative beginning (2 measures), note-against-note (6 measures)
Rehearsal D: Interlude introduces new choral and accompanimental ostinatos
Rehearsal E: Ostinato (4 measures), animated homophony (4 measures)
Rehearsal F: Countermelody
Rehearsal G: Animated homophony (4 measures), note-against-note (4 measures) (Note similarity with rehearsal C after opening to provide unity.)
Rehearsal H: Note-against-note

Let There Be Peace on Earth (arr.
**H. Ades.) Music contained in
Appendix II.**

The sections in the song *Let There Be Peace on Earth*, like most of those in *Sing a Rainbow*, are each eight measures. The overall structure for the arrangement is as follows:

ARRANGEMENT FORM	Intro	A	B	C	D	A	B	E	A'
TOTAL MEASURES	2	8	8	8	8	8	8	8	8
REHEARSAL LETTERS IN SCORE		A	B	C	D	E		F	

The following textures are found in this arrangement:

Rehearsal A: Unison, with figuration
Rehearsal B: Unison, with figuration
Rehearsal C: Note-against-note with figuration
Rehearsal D: Note-against-note with figuration
Rehearsal E: Canon (exact for eight measures, modified for eight measures)
Rehearsal F: Note-against-note

ARRANGING EXERCISES

1. Arrange *Magic Penny* for SA utilizing primarily note-against-note and animated homophonic textures. In the final eight measures (the return of A) experiment with imitation and short figurations. Do not write out an accompaniment, although you can assume one would be present to fill out the chords.

2. Write a countermelody to *Johnny Has Gone for a Soldier*. Consider whether the countermelody is best placed above or below the melody, taking into account the range of this source melody. Also investigate the possibility of imitation in a subsequent verse setting of this tune.

3. Practice composing a longer figuration in a setting of the spiritual *Were You There*. A text fragment should be used with the figuration. Apply another type of textural treatment in the last eight measures of this spiritual.

4. Compose an ostinato to be used in counterpoint against the folk melody *My Horses Ain't Hungry*. Use a text fragment that fits in with the original text. Also experiment with canon at various time intervals (starting with one measure). At what point in the melody will canon no longer be effective? What melodic factors have caused this to happen?

CHAPTER SIX

MODULATION

ONE OF THE MOST IMPORTANT DECISIONS THE ARRANGER MAKES in the early stages of planning is the choice of original key and the possibility for key change during the course of the arrangement. The original key is chosen after careful comparison of the range of the source melody with the range of the particular voice classifications in the arrangement. The source melody should typically lie in the middle or most comfortable singing *tessitura* of the highest voice part which will be assigned the melody, allowing some additional range above and below the melody for a countermelody, descant, or other contrapuntal line, or possible key change.

PURPOSE AND LOCATION

Modulation in the choral arrangement provides contrast and contributes to dramatic effect. Modulations normally appear near the end of the arrangement when there is a need for more variety and when the arranger wishes to signal that the climax and ending are near. Specific locations where modulations should take place relate to the form of the source melody. Three typical source melody forms with typical modulation location are given below.

Strophic   In a strophic setting, modulation can take place between any verses. Usually it is reserved to set off the last verse and signal the end of the piece.

AABA   With the AABA form, modulation occurs between the B and the last A. Although some arrangements exist with no repetition of any part of the AABA form, frequently either the entire AABA is repeated in the arrangement with some variation, or only the last two parts (BA) are repeated. In either case the modulation is normally reserved for the final statement of A.

Medley   Arrangements which combine two or more songs frequently employ modulation between the songs to set them apart and to allow for range changes in the source melodies.

A general guideline that is clear in all of the above models is that most modulations in choral arrangements take place at the point of a significant cadence at the end of a section.

KEY CHOICE

Since a primary reason for modulation is to heighten dramatic effect, most modulations tend to move to a higher rather than a lower key. The range of the source melody is a primary factor in considering the pitch level to which the modulation will ascend. Most typical is ascent by minor second (half-step) or major second (whole-step). Other choices are ascent up a minor third or, less frequently, a perfect fourth or fifth. Although the subdominant and dominant keys are closely related to the tonic (there is only one chromatic difference in their key signatures), the range difference makes these key choices impractical for most melodies. Key change up a minor or major second or a minor third usually involves change to a distant key (key signature difference of more than one chromatic), but a small change in range. It should be noted that choral modulations to higher keys normally keep the same mode as the original key—major to major tonality or minor to minor tonality. Distant relationships are made less harsh by careful application of a limited number of modulation types.[1]

On occasion, modulation in the choral arrangement may be to a lower key. Such key choice might reflect a somber text or sudden sad ending to the source melody. This descent usually involves movement down a minor or major second or perhaps a minor third.

TYPES OF MODULATION

There are only a few basic types of modulation, distinguished by the interaction of pitches at the point in the music when the key changes. The diversity and effectiveness of modulations, however, are largely dependent upon rhythm, texture,

---

[1]These principles do not apply in modulations involved in medleys—see p. 91

dynamics, and tempo. Therefore, as the various types of modulations are discussed, focusing upon the element of pitch in bringing about the modulation, the reader is urged to note the role of these other parameters, as well as how the essential style of the arrangement is maintained.

Pivot Chord Modulation

In music of the classical tradition, modulation is often produced within a phrase by means of a chord diatonic to both the original key and the new key that is used as a "pivot" or common chord between the two keys. For example, in modulating from the key of F major to the key of B♭ major, a g minor triad (serving as a ii chord in the first key and a vi chord in the second) is one of several chords that could be used as a pivot.

This type of modulation creates a smooth and subtle change of key. Because the arranger's purpose in changing keys is usually for sudden, dramatic effect, pivot chord modulation is rarely employed. The one place pivot chord modulation might be appropriate is in an interlude (discussed later in this chapter), where its subtlety may be desirable.

Chromatic Inflection

Modulation by chromatic inflection involves the alteration of a pitch by means of accidentals, so that the first key is denied and the new key is suggested. Since most modulations are upward, this alteration usually involves raising a pitch or pitches to form members of the V^7 chord in the new key. The motion is smooth in that the altered voices move chromatically stepwise, yet the new key may be distantly related, and thus the needed freshness is achieved.

The arrangement of *Go Tell It on the Mountain* excerpted in Example 6–1 is in the format of alternating chorus and verse. Chromatic modulation up a *half step* is employed between large sections as follows:

Key of D♭ major: Chorus
                  Verse
                  Chorus
            Modulation
Key of D major: Verse
                  Chorus
            Modulation
Key of E♭ major: Chorus

The above keys were decided upon because the final key of E♭ major puts the sopranos' highest pitch (g^2) at the top of their range and causes the baritone (or alto) soloist at the end of the arrangement to sustain a high $e♭$—in his (or her) brightest register. Working backwards, then, the key of D♭ major was selected to begin the arrangement.

Example 6–1. Traditional (arr. by P. Sjolund): *Go Tell It on the Mountain*

At the point of the first modulation, shown in Example 6–1, the task is to move smoothly from the D♭ chord, with which the D♭ major section cadences, to an A^7 chord, which will act as the V^7 of the new key of D major. Note that the entire chorus sings the pitch $a♭$ and then $a♮$ on beats 2 and 3 of the excerpt's second measure, thus creating the chromatic inflection.

The accompaniment accomplishes many tasks in this example.

1. It completes the cadence (V^7-I) in D♭ major to close that section.

2. It reinforces the chorus' chromatic motion ($a♭$ to $a♮$).

3. It sounds the new dominant (A^7) in root position to strengthen the motion into D major. (This root motion, down a diminished fourth, is difficult to anticipate aurally and thus is best left out of the vocal parts.)

4. It anticipates the soloist's pick-up note, providing a secure entrance.

5. Along with the chorus, it provides rhythmic motion into the new key.

Chromatic inflection is also frequently used to modulate up a *whole step*. In Example 6–2, the first section cadences in the key of F major. This is followed by a chord built on the sixth scale degree d, which diatonically would be a minor chord but because of the chromatic inflection (f becomes $f♯$) becomes a V^7 chord in the new key of G major.

Because the arrangement is geared to a young choir (SSCB), the voices rest while the modulation is prepared in the accompaniment. However, every attempt

Example 6–2. Riley and Wilson: *The Good Time Singers*

is made to keep the pitch *d* "fresh," since that is the sopranos' first note in the pick-up and downbeat in the new key. The accompaniment achieves this by waiting until the very last moment to sound the *d* pitch (even though the *f*♯ inflection was made on the downbeat of the third measure). Then the *d* finally sounds clearly, to facilitate a secure vocal entrance. From the vocal activity and piano octaves which prevail in this last section in G major, it is clear that the modulation serves to signal and prepare the verve and energy of the final chorus.

Common Tone Modulation

As the name implies, a modulation can be made between two quite-distant keys, using only one pitch which is common to structurally important chords (namely I and V) in both keys. For example, in C major, the pitch *c* is the root of the I chord. By sustaining or repeating that pitch in one voice to maintain orientation, the chorus could shift to an A♭ (as, say, I in that key), where the pitch *c* becomes reinterpreted as the third of the chord (Ex. 6–3).

Example 6–3.

This *c* is the only pitch common to the two sonorities and thus the modulation is dramatic. If the arranger had wished to modulate to the key of D♭ major, the A♭ chord could be thought of as V in that key, and then could become V⁷ by the addition of the pitch *g*♭ (Ex. 6–4).

Example 6–4.

Modulation up a major third can also be produced by means of a common tone—for example, where the third of the tonic chord in the original key becomes the root of the tonic chord in the new key (Ex. 6–5a). However, because it is not common for a section to end with the melody on the third of the tonic chord, adjustments may have to be made in the soprano part, such as: (1) altering the melody so that the sopranos sing the melody but do end on the third of the tonic chord (Ex. 6–5b); or (2) putting the melody in a lower voice so that it can end on the tonic pitch while the sopranos move to the third of the tonic chord (Ex. 6–5c).

Example 6–5a.

Example 6–5b.

Example 6–5c.

    Another way to effect this key relationship by common tone modulation is to employ the accompaniment, as in Example 6–6.

    In the excerpt's third measure, the accompaniment provides the plagal cadence (IV_4^6-I) to the previous section. The $g\sharp$ is the third of the I chord in E major, but is tied over and becomes reinterpreted as the root (enharmonically spelled) of the I chord in the key of A♭ major. This relationship allows a modulation up a major third (enharmonic).

    Note that in all illustrations of common tone modulation, the common tone is the top pitch of the sonority. This provides the greatest aural bridge between the two tonalities, while allowing the chords beneath to shift dramatically and "recolor" the common tone. Also that, while the enharmonic respelling (four sharps to four flats) creates an awkward notational shift, the new key of A♭ major is certainly more manageable than its "sharped" equivalent, the key of G♯ major.

Example 6–6. Traditional (arr. C. Forsberg): *Sing Praise to God*

Example 6–7. Spiritual (arr. F. F. Swift): *Ezekiel Saw de Wheel*

Direct Modulation

Direct modulation involves moving from one key to the next without an intervening pitch inflection or common sonority to prepare the new key. For this reason it is the most abrupt of the modulation types discussed here.

In Example 6–7, the first section cadences clearly in G major. Then, with no preparation, the next section begins up a half step in the key of A♭ major. The *fermata* reinforces the closure in the first key and creates a demand for a certain surprise in order to regenerate the arrangement's energy level. This demand is met by the *forte* entrance of the entire chorus on *e*♭ (remote to the key of G major). Of course, singing the *e*♭ in unison is not only dramatic but necessary, as the voice leading into that pitch is particularly awkward in the tenor and bass parts. The piano accompaniment, designated as optional in the arrangement, reinforces the voice parts.

Because of its wrenching effect, direct modulation occurs frequently in contemporary popular music, particularly rock music, to break the monotony of the simple harmonic progression while maintaining the propulsion created by the intensely syncopated rhythms.

Example 6–8 modulates from D minor, through the D♯ minor chord, to E minor in a direct fashion. The technique is intensified further by the syncopated placement of the D♯ minor seventh chord and the strict parallel motion in all voices. The modulation is manageable for the chorus because the accompaniment moves alone to the D♯ minor seventh chord, and then the *d*♯ pitch serves as the leading tone to the *e* on the downbeat of the E minor section. Tonal interest is achieved without stepping outside of the simple triadic vocabulary of this style of music.

Technical Considerations

In general, the simpler the voice leading in the choral parts, the more secure the performance of a modulation. It bears repeating that in writing for young voices the arranger might rest the voices while the piano accompaniment provides the modulation. In subtler settings, however, the chorus can be used to great effect to help bring about the modulation. *A cappella* settings are the extreme example of this, in which great care must be taken in voice leading so that intonation does not suffer. Essential voice leading involved in SATB settings of the various types of modulations are given in Example 6–9.

When a section of an arrangement is in a new key, a change of key signature is required, as illustrated in all of the examples in this chapter. The notational procedure is as follows:

1. The change of key signature should not be made until the beginning of the new section. Accidentals should be used with pick-up notes and other chromatic alterations before that point.

Example 6–8. Johnston (arr. A. Billingsley): *Long Train Running*

Example 6–9. Essential voice leading for typical ascending modulations in SATB settings. (Voicing may vary according to the chord tone in the melody.)

a. Chromatic inflection up a half step.   **b.** Chromatic inflection up a whole step.

c. Chromatic inflection up a minor third.   **d.** Common tone modulation—motion down a major third to V of new key.

e. Common tone modulation up a minor third.

f. Common tone modulation up a major third.

g. Direct modulation up a half step.

2. A double bar should be drawn to signal the change of key.

3. The new key signature should immediately follow the double bar. Should the new key occur at the beginning of a new score of music, the new key signature should also be indicated at the end of the previous score to prepare the performers.

CONTEXT OF THE MODULATION

The context of the modulation involves such factors as whether it is immediate or extended, and whether the modulation takes place in the voice parts alone, the accompaniment alone, or a combination of both.

Immediate Modulation

In an *immediate modulation* no additional music is added to that which would have existed if no modulation had taken place. The modulation therefore occurs in the cadence measures of the section immediately preceding the section which will be in the new key, or the new section simply begins in the new key without preparation (*direct modulation*). If the modulation occurs in the cadence measures, the modulatory agent is frequently chromatic inflection which is part of the dominant seventh chord of the new key.

Both a common tone connection and the chromatic inflection of the new key dominant are involved in the immediate modulation in Example 6–10. In this case the arranger simply substitutes the B dominant seventh chord for the tonic chord in the accompaniment, while the voices sing a unison *e♭*. The common tone connection (*e♭–d♯*) between the cadence note in the voices and the dominant of the new key makes a smooth key change. Note that the modulation takes place in the cadence measure and no additional measures are needed.

Extended Modulation

In an *extended modulation* an interlude is freely composed to effect the key change. This procedure is frequently employed with the strophic original source because it provides the additional musical benefit of breaking up the regularity of continuous verse repetition. The interlude may appear only in the accompanimental part or may combine the voices with the accompaniment. The interlude can be derived from a pitch-rhythm motif or text fragment from the source melody, or it might be newly composed. The interlude is interpolated after the cadence measure of the previous section and normally ends on the dominant seventh chord of the key which will begin the new section.

Example 6–11 illustrates an interlude exclusively in the keyboard that modulates down a minor third from F major to D major. The eight-measure interlude begins by sequencing a two-measure motive to set up key instability, and modulates through the chromatic inflection of the dominant seventh chord (A^7) of the new key. Although freely composed, the prominent quarter-note, step-wise pitch motive in the interlude is clearly derived from the hymn tune. The interlude provides contrast to the arrangement by separating the first two verses of the strophic hymn.

In the interlude of Example 6–12, the voices present a new rhythmic motif to provide contrasting musical material between verses 2 and 3 in this strophic spiritual. The text in the interlude leads up to the new subject treated in verse 3, rather than reworking text material from the previous verse. The modulation ascends a fourth

Example 6–10. Traditional (arr. J. Carter): *Oh, Dear! What Can the Matter Be?*

Example 6–11. Traditional (arr. F. Williams): *Praise the Lord, Ye Heavens Adore Him*

Example 6–12. Traditional (arr. R. Smith): *The Old Ship of Zion*

to the subdominant (F major) of the tonic (C major) and is effected by the introduction of the chromatic inflection ($b\flat$) which is part of the dominant seventh (C^7) of the new key (F major).

Medley

Some choral arrangements consist of two or more different songs which are pieced together into a cohesive setting. Typically the songs in a medley are in different keys to account for differences in range and to set off each song. Modulations which connect the songs in a medley are usually immediate, since there is already sufficient contrast present with the song variety.

Example 6–13 is characteristic of this approach. The song *You're a Grand Old Flag* in the key of Ab major is immediately followed by *America the Beautiful* in the key of C major. These keys allow the ranges of the respective melodies to be $e\flat^1$–$e\flat^2$ and e^1–e^2. The arranger chose to modulate immediately in the cadence measure of *You're a Grand Old Flag* by introducing the dominant seventh chord

Example 6–13. Traditional (arr. G. Grier and L. Everson): *Dancing with Uncle Sam*

Keep your eye on the grand old flag! ____ O   beau - ti - ful   for   spa - cious skies

(G^7) of the new key in the second half of the measure as a chromatic inflection
and then repeating the chord as the pick-up to the second song. Both voice parts
and accompaniment participate in this key change. The voicing of the G^7 chord in
the chorus is carefully chosen to lead logically into the beginning of *America the
Beautiful*.

ARRANGING EXERCISES

The following exercises draw upon the tune *This Train*, found in its entirety in
Appendix I.

1. Continue the *a cappella* SATB setting below, modulating up a half step.
Then continue in the new key as suggested by the soprano part given.

This train   is   bound   for glo - ry,   this train

This   train is   bound   for glo - ry,   this   train

(E♭ maj. chord)

This train   don't   car - ry   no gam - blers

2. In the following SATB setting, modulate up a whole step using transitional material in one or two of the lower voices. Write an accompaniment which supports the transitional material. Continue in the new key as suggested by the soprano part given.

3. Given the following SA setting in which the melody remains in the alto part, create a common tone modulation such that, in the new key, the first pitch of the given soprano melody becomes the root of the tonic chord (you will have to provide the new key signature). Add an accompaniment which reinforces the modulation, and write an alto part for the last two measures of the excerpt.

4. Create an SATB setting with accompaniment, using direct modulation, as dictated by the chord symbols in the excerpt below. (Only the final two measures of the source tune are given here, the second measure being part of the modulatory process.)

5. Following the excerpt below, write an interlude involving the piano (or piano with voices) which modulates up a minor third using any of the modulating procedures studied in this chapter. Be sure to draw upon material from the source tune.

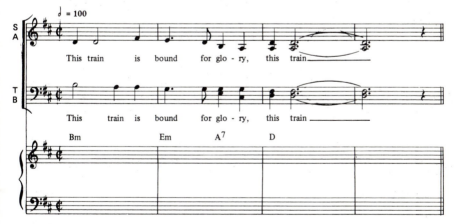

6. In arranging a medley for young voices, modulate in the excerpt below from the key of D major to the key of G major, relying primarily upon the accompaniment. Then begin *I've Been Workin' on the Railroad* (in unison or two treble parts) in the new key.

CHAPTER SEVEN

INTRODUCTIONS
AND ENDINGS

THE ARRANGER NEEDS TO CONSIDER CAREFULLY the musical presentation of beginnings and endings, for they must prepare the listener for the main body of the setting and also conclude the setting in such a way as to leave the listener with a sense of finality and satisfaction.

Introductions serve the two-fold musical purpose of establishing the scope, style, and mood for the arrangement while preparing the singers for the first statement of the opening melody. Endings, on the other hand, have the more general purposes of signaling the conclusion of the arrangement and providing appropriate emphasis on the final musical and textual ideas. Care must be taken by the arranger to allow introductions and endings to balance the body of the setting and never to overshadow it.

Introductions and endings may be instrumental, vocal *(a cappella)*, or vocal with accompaniment. These different categories of texture will be seen to be associated with different kinds of introductions and endings. The descriptions that follow focus on the most common of these and are not intended to be all-inclusive.

Contrary to what might initially seem logical, introductions and endings are normally composed after the main body of the arrangement. One reason for this is the fact that introductions are often based on accompanimental or melodic treatments which occur in the body of the arrangement. Also, the arranger by then has a better feeling for the overall mood and dramatic direction of the arrangement and can better integrate the introduction to fit a common overall goal. A logical sequence for incorporating the writing of introductions and endings into the overall arrangement is presented in Chapter 8 ("Planning the Arrangement").

INTRODUCTIONS DIRECTLY DERIVED
FROM THE ARRANGEMENT

The most common types of introductions are based on musical materials which appear prominently in the body of the arrangement. Most of these are purely instrumental, thus fulfilling the role of providing pitch reference for the initial vocal entrance.

Introductions Derived
from the First Phrase

Frequently, introductions state a portion of the first phrase of music. This not only unifies the arrangement but also states the important melodic pitches of the first phrase, so the singers can orient themselves for their initial entrance. Sometimes the melodic and harmonic material at the end of the phrase are altered to cadence on a pitch that leads logically into the first vocal entrance.

The introduction in Example 7–1 has all these qualities. Melodically, it starts out identically to the vocal entrance, but the time values lengthen and the introduction ends on f^1 to lead logically into the vocal entrance. The introduction also serves to establish the tonic as well as the texture and rhythm of the keyboard accompaniment.

Introductions Derived
from a Subsequent Phrase

Many introductions are based on subsequent or ending phrases of the main melody. This is seen in multi-verse settings where a cadence phrase leads logically into the repeat of the first phrase of the melody. No alteration of the melodic material is expected here because the cadence phrase of a melody usually ends on the tonic note, an easy referential pitch for phrase beginnings.

Example 7–2 utilizes the final phrase of *Wassail, Wassail* as an introduction. This material establishes the tonic clearly, emphasizing the anacrusic flavor of the melody, and ends on the tonic for easy reference to the dominant-tonic beginning of the melody. The accompanimental style has a bit more motion than the sustained style accompaniment at the beginning of the choral section, providing both a secure tempo and rhythmic vitality.

The introduction seen in Example 7–3 shows a vocal treatment using the final phrase of the melody for *I'm Just a Poor Wayfarin' Stranger*. Since this is an *a*

Example 7–1. Traditional (arr. H. Wilson and W. Ehret): *Winds through the Olive Tree*

Harry Wilson and Walter Ehret, *Prentice-Hall Choral Series,*
Book 2, Englewood Cliffs, NJ, 1960. Reprinted by permission.

Example 7–2. Traditional (arr. H. Wilson and W. Ehret): *Wassail, Wassail*

Harry Wilson and Walter Ehret, *Prentice-Hall Choral Series*,
Book 2, Englewood Cliffs, NJ, 1960. Reprinted by permission.

Example 7–3. Traditional (arr. L. Kyelson): *I'm Just a Poor Wayfarin' Stranger*

© 1963 by Belwin, Inc. Reprinted with permission.

cappella arrangement, there is no possibility of using an accompanying instrument. The options open to the arranger are to use a solo voice (as here), one section of the chorus, or all voices, or to eliminate an introduction altogether. The solo voice helps to set the mood for the prominent melody in the soprano part and to establish tonic and the starting tonic note clearly. It also personalizes the poignant text.

Introductions Derived from the Accompaniment

Accompaniments which have catchy rhythmic patterns with faster tempos can also be used as the basis for an introduction. Such accompanimental patterns must quickly set the mood, establish tonic, and provide easy pitch reference for the opening vocal entrance.

An excellent illustration of this type is seen in Example 7–4. Here the repeated accompanimental pattern is set against the tonic-fifth pedal in the left hand. The pattern catches the spirit and forward motion of the melody and also makes it easy for the singers to enter on the tonic note.

Example 7–4. Traditional (arr. K. K. Davis): *As It Fell upon a Night*

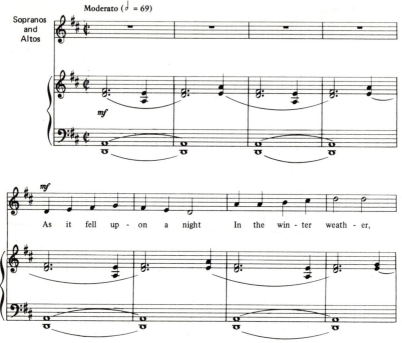

Introductions That Combine Functions

More extensive introductions may combine prominent melodic material with portions of accompanimental patterns. The advantage of this treatment is the possibility of highlighting more than one musical aspect of the main body of the arrangement in a longer context, while more securely setting the mood and building suspense for the initial vocal entrance.

The introduction in Example 7–5 begins by stating a two-measure fragment from an interior phrase of this familiar folk song in the right hand of the keyboard accompaniment. The fragment is then moved to the left hand for a second statement, followed by several repetitions of the keyboard accompanimental pattern, clearly establishing opening pitches and meter for the vocalists.

Example 7–5. Traditional (arr. J. Carter): *Oh Dear! What Can the Matter Be?*

© 1982 by Somerset Press. Reprinted with permission.

ENDINGS DIRECTLY DERIVED
FROM THE ARRANGEMENT

An ending serves as a gradual conclusion of the arrangement, avoiding an abrupt cessation at the end of the final phrase of the melody, and focuses additional emphasis on a final musical or textual idea. For this reason, endings typically repeat the last phrase of the setting or concentrate on an idea that was prominent near the end. Endings are usually vocal with accompaniment (if an accompanied arrangement) to link closely with the closing ideas of the source melody.

Example 7–6. Traditional (arr. M. S. Vance): *Pretty Saro*

Endings That Repeat
the Last Phrase

The simplest ending repeats the last phrase of music. The repetition need not, however, be exact. Variation can be added through change in texture, text, or harmony, or by introducing a *ritardando*. The essential point is that the principal melodic idea remains the same.

The ending of *Pretty Saro* (Ex. 7–6) exemplifies this approach. The final phrase of the melody, originally stated in the men's voices, is, in the ending, moved to the soprano. Most of the text is dropped to emphasize the dream suggested in the text, and the harmony is changed to a series of diatonic seventh chords to coloristically support the mood. The *poco a poco ritardando* also serves to give finality to the ending.

Endings That Feature Rhythmic
Augmentation

Another straightforward ending procedure is to slow down the final phrase by doubling or even quadrupling the rhythmic values. This may take place as the last phrase is stated or may involve repetition of a portion of the last phrase. The precise number of notes which are rhythmically altered depends primarily on the text. The general guideline is to include a complete textual thought and augment the rhythmic values of the notes so that one or two notes occur in each measure. The effect is that of broadening or even retarding the tempo.

Example 7–7b illustrates a doubling of the rhythmic values from the final measures of *Early in the Morning*. This material recurs several times earlier in the arrangement as the concluding phrase of the chorus (Ex. 7–7a), therefore requiring little preparation as a final phrase in longer (augmented) values. The melody notes in the soprano are also altered to end high in the tessitura as part of a dramatic conclusion. Compare the augmented six-measure version (Ex. 7–7b) with the original four-measure setting (Ex. 7–7a) to observe not only this choral treatment but also the role of the accompaniment in achieving a sense of finality.

The Tag Ending

Sometimes an arrangement requires only a brief punctuation to signal the end. The term *tag* signifies such a short ending and is used in various styles of choral music for this purpose. In popular styles, most endings are called *tags,* and may utilize a number of techniques, including the previously discussed last phrase repetition and rhythmic augmentation. In more traditional styles, a tag is usually a very short idea, less than a phrase in length. One possible tag is a single chord in the chorus and accompaniment to a single word of text such as "Hey!" in the measure after the final cadence. Another possibility is a measure of musical punctuation related to the text or music of the source tune. The tag illustrated in Example

Example 7–7a. Traditional (arr. J. Carter): *Early in the Morning*

7–8 uses a one-measure melodic fragment from *What Can the Matter Be?* followed by single bass-note downbeats in the accompaniment. The effect is a rather abrupt punctuation that tells the listener that the arrangement is over.

FREELY COMPOSED INTRODUCTIONS AND ENDINGS

Arrangers may choose to use musical materials for introductions or endings which are less closely related to the musical source. These freely-composed sections may be based on rhythmic patterns, harmonic patterns, or textual references to the main body of the arrangement.

Imitative Beginnings or Endings

One of the recurring textures chosen for freely-composed introductions or endings is imitation. The arranger begins with a short motif that has either a musical or a textual connection to the source and then imitates it throughout the vocal parts. For a detailed description of the technique of imitation, the reader is directed to Chapter 10. Note particularly the imitative beginning to the spiritual *Ain't That Good News*, Example 10–13 of that chapter.

Example 7–7b. Traditional (arr. J. Carter): *Early in the Morning*

Example 7–8. Traditional (arr. J. Carter): *Oh Dear! What Can the Matter Be?*

In Example 7–9, the word "hallelujah" from the preceding chorus forms the basis for the freely composed imitative ending. In this setting a four-note motive rises from the bass voice to the soprano, followed by a brief note-against-note section. The text serves as the source for the ending, but the rhythmic motive is freely composed and does not relate to the final phrase.

Other Freely Composed
Introductions or Endings

Arrangers also compose totally independent musical material for use in introductions and endings, retaining only such general features as tempo and tonality. Frequently, an original idea may be used as the basis for both introduction and ending to help achieve unity.

The introduction to *Grandma's Feather Bed* (Ex. 7–10a) is freely composed for three measures in both voices and accompaniment, followed by four measures

Example 7–9. Traditional (arr. R. H. Smith): *The Old Ship of Zion*

Example 7–10a. J. Connor (arr. D. Riley and D. Wilson): *Grandma's Feather Bed*

Example 7–10b. J. Connor (arr. D. Riley and D. Wilson): *Grandma's Feather Bed*

of the principal accompanimental pattern leading into the first verse. The "tang, dig-a-dang, dang" motive sets the country flavor from the outset of the arrangement, borrowing some rhythm patterns from the source melody. However, it comes across as an independent melodic and textual idea that does not occur in the main body of the arrangement.

The ending of the arrangement restates the same "tang, dig-a-dang, dang" idea ending with the title text (see Example 7–10b). This rounds off the arrangement nicely, unifying the beginning and ending yet setting these portions off from everything else.

The same general arranging principles are found in Examples 7–11a and 7–11b. The introduction to *Corner of the Sky* consists of two separate sections which are not directly derived from the body of the arrangement. The first six measures present a theme in the keyboard accompaniment that sets the mood and signals to the listener that rhythmic syncopation will be important in the music that is ahead. The remaining two measures present a new syncopated accompanimental pattern along with background "oo" in the vocal parts.

The ending (Ex. 7–11b) reverses these two ideas to form an arch-like symmetrical large-scale form in the introduction-ending relationship. The first four measures use the "oo" material in the vocal parts against the syncopated figure in the acompaniment (same as measures 7–8 in Example 7–11a). The final three measures restate the theme from the very beginning of the introduction, thus rounding off the setting.

The general arranging concept demonstrated by Examples 7–10 and 7–11 is that when musical material is newly composed for the introduction, it should be balanced by recurrence at the ending. From a practical standpoint, it is recommended that the arranger gain experience with the simpler style introductions and endings before trying more creative, freely-composed types which require considerable experience in composition.

ARRANGING EXERCISES

1. Write a two-part (SA) accompanied introduction for the folk song *I Know Where I'm Going*. Derive the introduction from the first phrase of the tune.

2. Write a two-part (SA) accompanied introduction for *Gypsy Rover*. Derive the introduction from any phrase other than the first phrase of the tune.

3. Compose a piano introduction for *Oh, Sinner Man*. Remember to prepare for the vocal entrance on the dominant pitch.

4. Compose a two-part (SA) ending for *This Little Light of Mine* that involves augmenting the rhythmic values in the last phrase of the spiritual.

Example 7–11a. S. Schwartz (arr. J. Cacavas): *Corner of the Sky*

Example 7–11b. S. Schwartz (arr. J. Cacavas): *Corner of the Sky*

Got to find my cor-ner— of the sky—

CHAPTER EIGHT

PLANNING
THE ARRANGEMENT

CREATIVITY IN ARRANGING IS MORE A MATTER of logically combining choral materials than a process of spontaneous creation that begins at measure 1 and proceeds to the end of the arrangement. What initially may seem like an almost insurmountable undertaking can be broken down into a logical series of procedures that even a relatively inexperienced musician can use to create a *unified* choral arrangement. As the arranger gains experience in handling choral materials and organizing arrangements, some portions of the planning process become automatic, and the arranger can quickly assimilate materials and move quickly to the writing phrase. In this chapter, an outline of this planning process will be discussed in detail, followed by an application of this process to a complete arrangement.

INITIAL CONSIDERATIONS REGARDING
PERFORMANCE GROUP
AND MUSICAL SOURCE

Many arrangements are written for a specific performing group, often by its conductor. Such groups might vary anywhere from the elementary school two-part choir to the high school chorus to the all-women's or all-men's section of the local choral society to the church choir. The arranger needs to know not only the typical voice ranges for the intended singers but also the strengths and weaknesses of the particular group in terms of range, rhythm, pitch, and voice independence, and how that information will affect the arrangement.

An equally important consideration is the selection of a musical source for the arrangement. Initially, the arranger needs to decide on a general style, such as folk, spiritual, popular, or hymn tune. In selecting the source melody, attention must be paid both to the suitability of text and to the vocal demands of the music with respect to the maturity of the choral group.

DETAILED STUDY
OF THE MUSICAL SOURCE

The arranger needs to have a thorough understanding of the musical features of the source melody as well as the emotional and expressive features of the text. These early considerations begin to shape both the scope and variety of treatment that will emerge in the subsequent stages of arrangement planning.

Text

The text of the source melody provides the most significant information relative to the overall mood and the degree to which change takes place over the course of the song. The following series of questions relative to the text may help to focus on these issues as preliminary considerations for the arrangement.

1. Who is speaking?
2. To whom is he or she speaking?
3. Where and under what circumstances?
4. What is the overriding message?
5. Are there connotations of anger, sadness, bitterness, reflection, or happiness in the tone of voice of the person speaking?
6. Do any of the above change from verse to verse?

Melodic Form

Another important factor which will influence the arrangement is the form of the source melody. Three particular forms provide the organizational basis for most of the source material used for choral arrangements.

Sectional   Most popular literature uses the framework of AABA (or sometimes ABA). The four sections of AABA normally have separate lines of text and are each eight measures in length (giving a total of thirty-two measures). The initial A idea is usually repeated, followed by a contrasting B section, and finishing with a turn of A. Examples of the form are *Button Up Your Overcoat* and the Beatles' *Yesterday*. ABA and other sectional forms follow similar eight-measure groupings.

Strophic   Many folk songs follow a general strophic pattern, where a single melody of eight or sixteen measures is repeated several times as the verses *(strophes)* of the text unfold a tale. Examples of the strophic type are *John Henry* and *Down in the Valley*.

Strophic with refrain   Also found as a basis for many folk songs, the strophic-with-refrain design follows each verse with a refrain that repeats a melody and text. Typically, a verse might be eight measures in length, followed by an eight-measure refrain. *The Erie Canal* and *Sweet Betsy from Pike* are good examples of this type of form.

Pitch and Rhythmic Organization

Another consideration is the organization of pitch and rhythm in the melody. Certain types of pitch and rhythmic activity can have a significant effect on the treatment of texture, accompaniment and other musical elements in the arrangement. Answering the following questions helps to begin the process of deciding how various sections in the arrangement will be treated musically.

Melody

1. How wide is the range?
2. Is the melody essentially conjunct or disjunct?
3. Is there a perceivable contour?

Rhythm

1. What is the appropriate tempo?
2. Is there a preponderance of slower or faster rhythmic values?
3. Is there rhythmic continuity?
4. Are there continual breaks in the rhythmic flow?

PLANNING THE OVERALL FORM
OF THE ARRANGEMENT

The overall form of the arrangement will be governed primarily by the form of the source melody. Within this natural constraint, the arranger still needs to have a sense of the total length in terms of the number of measures or number of phrase statements or repetitions at the appropriate tempo for the source melody. The following is provided as a general guideline to large-scale arrangement form based on the form of the source melody.

Sectional (AABA)

The body of the arrangement may simply contain the four sections of the source melody, particularly if the tempo is slow. In a moderate or faster tempo, either the entire AABA form can be repeated, or only the final BA can be repeated with contrasting treatment. Since most sections of the AABA form contains eight measures, the overall length of the body of the arrangement will be 32, 48, or 64 measures.

Strophic

The body of the strophic arrangement is determined by the number of verses in the source. Sometimes, folk songs have far more verses than would be practical to include within the boundaries of an arrangement. In this case, the arranger has to decide which verses may be superfluous to the overall intent of the text, but still must maintain the minimum verses of text for preserving the story. If each verse is only eight measures long, anywhere from four to eight verses (32 to 64 measures) can easily be included in the overall form.

Strophic with Refrain

As with the strophic form, the body of the strophic-with-refrain arrangement is determined by the number of verses in the source, and likewise, some verses may need to be eliminated for the sake of brevity. Since the typical strophic-with-refrain source totals sixteen measures, most arrangements include three to four verses with refrain (48 to 64 measures). Variety may be introduced in the arrangement by skipping an occasional refrain and linking verses which are unified by text.

THE CONTRIBUTION OF MUSICAL
ELEMENTS TO FORM DELINEATION

Once the scope of the arrangement is determined, the principal musical elements of *choral texture, accompaniment, dynamics, key change,* and *tempo change* need to be considered carefully to see how they may contribute to the form. The form of the arrangement will be determined by the degree to which these and other musical elements change or stay the same. There may be times when all the principal elements will change from one section to the next; but more often, *some* elements will remain the same between sections to achieve unity.

The following discussion is a summary of the ways in which the principal musical elements change between the main sections of an arrangement. Much more detailed discussion of these elements appears on the chapters on two-, three-, and four-part arranging, accompaniment, and modulation.

Texture

Texture is the most important element of change in the choral arrangement. Almost all adjacent sections should differ in texture—keeping in mind that too many changes can make a piece fragmented or disjointed. As a general guideline, use one texture treatment for four to eight measures in a slow tempo and eight to sixteen measures in a faster tempo. Simple unison or homophonic textures are used in the initial portions of the arrangement, leading to more complex contrapuntal applications later to help achieve a climax.

Accompaniment

The accompaniment is the next most important musical element for achieving formal contrast. The accompaniment can provide contrast in mood, key, tempo, meter, or style by immediate change, or through the use of interludes to separate sections. The important point is that the accompaniment will not change as frequently as the choral texture, thus providing unity as well as contrast.

Dynamics

Dynamics change between sections somewhat less frequently than do texture or accompaniment, but variety in dynamic level is used to reflect changes in mood and text. Dynamic change can also occur *within* sections, where a *crescendo* or *decrescendo* might help project aspects of the text. If an arrangement has a climax at the end, the loudest dynamic level is reserved for this section.

Key

Key centers change much less frequently than either texture or accompaniment. Many arrangements contain no key change at all. When key change is used as a formal delineator, usually the final section or sections will change key by ascending a second or third above the original key. Occasionally, more than one tonality change will set off other sections of the arrangement.

Tempo

Tempo changes less frequently than the other principal elements. Although internal sections of the arrangement can be set off by tempo change, perhaps to highlight a poignant verse of text, more often the last verse or section of the arrangement is contrasted (usually slowed down) to help signal finality and climax.

APPLICATION OF MUSICAL ELEMENTS
TO SPECIFIC FORMS

The following applications represent typical ways in which these elements can be used to provide unity or contrast in the three source forms previously discussed.

Sectional (AABA)

Texture   Normally, a different texture distinguishes each section in this form. Simple unison or homophonic treatments appear at the beginning, leading to more complex textures toward the end. If the BA sections are repeated, one or both may restate the original texture, but more often, the final A will be different.

Accompaniment   The accompaniment will stay the same for some portions of a sectional form and vary for others. Typically, the opening A sections remain the same; B may contrast. If BA is repeated, the AABA may be unified by using a similar accompaniment, while the BA repetition is changed.

Dynamics   There is no set pattern for the application of dynamics to sectional form. Some sections undoubtedly will be contrasted; but more than any other element, dynamics will closely reflect the mood and expression of the text.

Key   The entire AABA is normally presented in one key. If BA is repeated, either both parts or, more often, the final A section may be in a new key.

Tempo   The entire initial presentation of AABA is also presented in one tempo. Any repetitions may be marked by tempo change.

Strophic

Texture   Each verse in strophic form is contrasted by texture, with a gradual change from more simple unison and other homophonic treatments to more complex contrapuntal applications. A restatement of an earlier texture may appear as part of the last verses.

Accompaniment   In strophic form, a consistent accompaniment may group certain verses; a changing one may provide contrast between verses. One possible plan might be to link two or three verses together in the initial part of the arrangement and separate the final verses to provide an acceleration toward the end.

Dynamics   Dynamic change occurs between most verses to reflect the overall mood and expression of the text.

Key   If key change is used, normally the final verse is set off to achieve a sense of climax.

Tempo   In strophic form, either the last verse, or a verse that has a text that needs particular highlighting, may be contrasted by tempo change.

Strophic with Refrain

Texture   As in the strophic form, adjacent verses contain different textures, with movement from simple to complex throughout the arrangement. The refrain will have the same texture throughout to provide unity. The final refrain may have some change to help signal climax and conclusion.

Accompaniment   In this form, verses are either grouped with the same accompaniment for unity, or changed to add contrast. The refrain normally has the same accompaniment each time.

Dynamics   As in strophic form, change of dynamics occurs between most verses reflecting the overall mood and expression of the text. The refrain is unified by maintaining one dynamic level.

Key   If key change is used, either the final verse and refrain or only the final refrain will contain key change.

Tempo   Either the last verse or the last refrain may be contrasted by tempo. If an internal verse requires tempo change for textual emphasis, the refrain which follows the verse will normally return to the original tempo.

ADDING INTRODUCTIONS AND ENDINGS

The possibility of including an introduction or an ending is only considered after the overall scope and specific form of the arrangement has been determined. At this time, the arranger has a feeling for the overall mood and dramatic direction of the piece and can decide if an introduction or ending can contribute to that form. A second, more practical, reason for considering introductions and endings at this time is that most of them are derived from choral or accompanimental material from the body of the arrangement, and the appropriate choice of musical materials is only known after the arrangement is planned. The specific practices for arranging introductions and endings is detailed in Chapter 7.

FINAL ASSEMBLY OF THE ARRANGEMENT

At this point, the complete scope, including the exact number of measures in each section, is set. The musical treatment for each section is known on either a general descriptive basis or in actual sketch form. Now the arranger assembles the pieces of the puzzle by writing out all the sections of the arrangement and combining them with care to allow for continuity and a natural flow between sections.

APPLYING THE PLANNING PROGRESSION
TO AN EXISTING ARRANGEMENT

The arrangement of John Carter's *Early in the Morning* for three-part mixed chorus (see Appendix II) is discussed below to illustrate the process of arrangement planning through the six stages as outlined in this chapter.

Considering the Type of Group

The arrangement of *Early in the Morning* is conceived for a three-part middle school chorus. Girls, and boys with unchanged voices, are assigned to the top two parts, and boys with changed voices, to the lower part. Since the singers are young, the lower part will need a fairly limited range $(c–d^1)$ and the upper parts should not go too high.

Detailed Study of the Musical Source and Text

The form of this source material (originally a sea chanty) is verse and refrain. There are six verses that center on the Christmas story. The first four verses present a question-and-answer format and cover different aspects surrounding the background of the story. The fifth and sixth verses change this format dramatically, suggesting the awe of seeing the baby in the manger and finally expressing the joy of the event. The refrain, consisting of an exuberant "alleluia," stays the same throughout.

The melodic material utilizes quick-moving quarter and eighth-note rhythmic values throughout. The melody has a range of an octave, with step motion predominant. The problematic aspect of the melodic structure is that the verse and refrain have almost identical melodies. This suggests that other musical elements besides the text are needed to separate refrain from verse.

Planning the Overall Form of the Arrangement

Since each verse and each refrain is eight measures long, the total of six verses with refrain is 96 measures. Balancing this potential length problem is the fact that the melody moves at a fast tempo in cut time. From a text standpoint, all the verses are really needed; one possible approach to cutting the length is to eliminate a refrain. Since the last two verses represent a significant change in text, the refrain can be omitted between these verses. That leaves a potential 88 measures before consideration of an introduction or ending.

THE CONTRIBUTORS OF MUSICAL ELEMENTS TO FORM DELINEATION

	TEXTURE	ACCOMPANIMENT	DYNAMICS	KEY	TEMPO
VERSE 1	Unison	Rhythmic	mf	d	𝅗𝅥 = 66
REFRAIN	Melody with figuration and note-against-note	Rhythmic	f	d	𝅗𝅥 = 66
VERSE 2	Melody with background	Rhythmic pattern	mf	d	𝅗𝅥 = 66
REFRAIN	Unchanged	—	—	—	—
VERSE 3	Two-voice ostinato and note-against-note	Homophonic	mf	d	𝅗𝅥 = 66
REFRAIN	Unchanged	—	—	—	—
VERSE 4	Unison	Homophonic with rhythmic punctuation	mp	d	𝅗𝅥 = 66

	TEXTURE	ACCOMPANIMENT	DYNAMICS	KEY	TEMPO
REFRAIN	Unchanged	—	—	—	—
VERSE 5	Note-against note sustained		mf	d	slower
(Refrain Omitted)					
VERSE 6	Two-voice note-against-note with ostinato	Rhythmic, and rhythmic pattern	f	d	$\downarrow$ = 66
REFRAIN	Unchanged, except alteration for ending in augmentation.				

Summary of Formal Treatment

Texture   Every verse contrasts. Simple textural beginning. Verse 4 reuses initial texture. Most complex texture appears at the end.

Accompaniment   Every verse contrasts. Simple beginning. Verse 4 reuses original accompaniment as well as texture. Verse 6 reuses the accompaniment from verses 1 and 2. The accompaniment is used as both a contrasting and a unifying element.

Dynamics   Every verse and refrain contrast, but the first three verses and verse 5 all use the same dynamic level. The quieter dynamics in verse 4 prepare for the key change in verse 5. The *forte* in verse 6 signals the climax.

Key change   No key change. D dorian mode throughout unifies the arrangement.

Tempo   Essentially a unifier, but verse 5 is set off by the only tempo contrast in the piece.

The arrangement is a cohesive whole with a combination of contrasting and unifying treatments. The simple beginning leads gradually to a section of extensive contrast (verse 5) and climax at the last verse.

Adding Introductions and Endings

A simple introduction in the piano which is derived from a portion of the first phrase plus the opening accompanimental pattern sets the mood and establishes the opening pitch for the singers. The already long arrangement does not require an additional ending. Instead, the last phrase of the final refrain is augmented to slow down the rhythmic activity and signal the conclusion.

CHAPTER NINE

THREE-PART ARRANGING

THE THREE-PART ARRANGEMENT PROVIDES AN EXCELLENT medium for continuing the development of arranging skills, since it expands many of the two-part arranging procedures discussed in Chapter 5, yet still restricts some of the complexities found in four-part settings. One of these restrictions is harmony, because not all chords can be fully expressed with three voices. For this reason and others—such as range—the three-part arrangement is usually accompanied by keyboard.

TYPICAL VOICE COMBINATIONS AND APPLICATIONS

Most three-part arrangements are scored for either SSA or SAB (SCB). The TTB or TBB three-part male designations are reserved for *divisi* sections of larger SATB choral works, since most all-male pieces are TTBB.

The most common all-female voice combination is SSA, although there are also arrangements for SA or SSAA. The primary consideration in setting either of these combinations is the rather high tessitura of $(f)g–g^2$ (a^2). Although this range provides a full two octaves for choral voicings, it still is placed high for the normal fundamental bass of the chord, which normally occurs between G and c^1. For most SSA or even SSAA arrangements, this fundamental bass for the harmony therefore occurs in the accompaniment, with the lowest voice either doubling the bass or sounding another pitch in the harmony. As explained later in this chapter, this tessitura restriction influences not only the texture choice but also the way in which the voices function within the texture.

The SAB texture is particularly useful in two common situations: in the choir with few male voices, as in church choirs and even some high schools, where separate soprano and alto parts are balanced by a single baritone part sung by all males; and in junior high school groups, where boys with voices in the process of changing—and perhaps some girls with lower voice ranges—sing the *cambiata* part, while boys with changed voices sing baritone (thus the designation SCB). In this latter application, the cambiata or middle part is carefully written with a narrow range and rhythmic simplicity. Many arrangements labeled SAB may also be performed by the SCB combination, but the conductor needs to examine the alto line carefully for range and rhythmic content. Contemporary arrangers frequently designate the three parts using the Roman numerals I, II, and III to allow the conductor to assign a variety of voice types to the voice parts. Voice parts I and II are in treble clef, and III is in bass clef. The discussion in this chapter will focus on both SSA and SAB combinations.

HOMOPHONIC TEXTURES

Note-against-Note

The note-against-note texture is used with melodies that have fairly active rhythmic patterns. The melody is always assigned to the top line, with the lower two parts filling in the harmony using the same rhythmic values as the melody. In the SSA application, this texture frequently utilizes parallel motion between the three parts, maintaining close voicing. The alto line cannot provide the fundamental line for the harmony, not only because of lack of lower range but also because it is parallel to the soprano; the fundamental bass is then assigned to the accompaniment.

Example 9–1 illustrates an SSA example in essentially parallel motion. The excerpt maintains a close voicing throughout, where the lower two parts are assigned the triad members which appropriately harmonize the soprano line. The fundamental bass for the harmony occurs in the left hand of the accompaniment and is independent of the alto part. The right hand of the keyboard part duplicates the choral parts and also adds a simple rhythmic figure for continuity. Although the parallel vocal treatment is appropriate for this SSA setting, it becomes tedious if overused or if it is not contrasted with other texture types.

In the SAB application, there is more frequent use of contrary motion and some change between open and close voicing, although open voicing predominates. Here the baritone part is often assigned the fundamental line for the harmony and therefore frequently duplicates the bass line of the accompaniment. Since it is not always possible to provide complete harmonies with three choral voices, the accompaniment

Example 9–1. Loewe (arr. C. Warnick): *Camelot*

By or - der, sum - mer lin - gers through Sep - tem - ber _____

By or - der, sum - mer lin - gers through Sep - tem - ber _____

By or - der, sum - mer lin - gers through Sep - tem - ber _____

plays an important role in filling out the harmony. An important arranging consideration is the relationship of the lowest voice of the choral texture to the bass line of the accompaniment.

The SAB setting in Example 9–2 contrasts with Example 9–1 in several ways. Contrary motion is used extensively between the soprano and baritone parts. Although arranged primarily in open voicing, close position chords in measures 6 and 8 provide variety. The baritone part relates closely to the bass line of the accompaniment; note that all downbeat pitches are identical, but as the baritone part continues the note-against-note rhythmic relationship on other beats, additional notes are sounded in this part to add harmonic variety and completeness and to provide interest and to make the line more singable through step connection. The keyboard contributes harmonic completeness and has little independence.

Animated Homophony

An animated homophonic texture is an expansion of the note-against-note texture where the added two voices are always below the melody, embellishing the chord tones of the note-against-note texture with additional pitches. This texture is frequently chosen to vary a melody that has already been presented in a more simple texture. The arranger is advised to first set a melody in a note-against-note texture, and then to add the embellishing tones for the animated homophony.

Example 9–3 shows the last verse of a setting of *The Holly and the Ivy* that utilizes this texture type for the culmination of the arrangement. The melody is clearly stated in the soprano, while the lower two voices fill in the basic harmony

Example 9–2. Traditional (arr. H. Wilson and W. Ehret): *Wind through the Olive Trees*

Harry Wilson and Walter Ehret, *Prentice-Hall Choral Series,*
Book 2, Englewood Cliffs, NJ, 1960. Reprinted by permission.

Example 9–3. Traditional (arr. R. Ringwald): *The Holly and the Ivy*

From the collection *Come Sing*, © 1959 Shawnee Press, Inc.,
Delaware Water Gap, PA 18327. Used by permission.

with eighth-note passing activity, often in parallel sixths. This example also illustrates a baritone line which is separate from the fundamental bass line of the keyboard
accompaniment.

Melody Line with Background
Vocal Texture

Frequently the arranger desires to highlight a melodic line in a single voice
part, relegating the remaining two voices to background harmonic support. Like
the animated homophonic approach, this texture is best used for short sections to
provide formal contrast. The melody most frequently occurs in either the soprano
or baritone, so the other two voices (alto and baritone or soprano and alto) can
easily be paired. These background voices are assigned single words of the text or
neutral syllables moving in longer rhythmic values than the melody. Each part in
the background vocal texture is usually simple so that the two parts together do not
overpower or distract from the melodic line. The subordinate lines must still make
''sense'' to the singers, so that they will stay involved emotionally.

In Example 9–4, the melody is assigned to the soprano I, while the soprano
II and alto are coupled in support. These parts are assigned the neutral syllable
''ah'' and duplicate the soprano text at cadence points. Harmonically, the supporting
voices duplicate pitches in the keyboard accompaniment. The fundamental bass for
the harmony is also found in the keyboard. Typical SSA close voicing is maintained
until the cadence at the end of the example.

Example 9–4. Loewe (arr. C. Warnick): *How to Handle a Woman*

For the first four measures of Example 9–5, the melody is placed in the baritone part, with the upper two parts paired in support, using chord tones and a text fragment (forming a complete thought) from the baritone. In the last four measures, the melody moves to the soprano, where it is accompanied by a note-against-note alto line and sustained tones in the baritone. The text for the baritone is a fragment from the melody; its pitch material is duplicated in the bass line of the accompaniment, providing the fundamental bass.

CONTRAPUNTAL TEXTURES

Countermelody

Three-part arrangements frequently feature a countermelody as a common type of contrapuntal texture. As described in Chapter 5, a countermelody is an independent line sounding against a given melody that maintains separate pitch, rhythm, and contour in its own line, but that is predominantly consonant with the original. In three-part textures, there are two general approaches to countermelody. The countermelody may be presented in a single line, while the other two voices are paired note-against-note, with the main melody occurring in the upper paired voice. Or the countermelody may itself be paired note-against-note with one of the other voices, while the remaining voice is assigned the melody. The countermelody appears above or below the original melody.

Either a text or a neutral vowel sound is assigned to the countermelody, depending on its rhythmic activity and its musical relationship to the original melody. Texts are frequently derived from, or closely related to, the original text, although a separate, unrelated text contributes to the independence of the countermelody and creates tension leading to the climax of the arrangement.

In Example 9–6, the soprano and alto pair together in a note-against-note setting of the traditional melody found in the soprano. The baritone countermelody in the first phrase complements the rhythm of the original melody, while in the second phrase it frequently duplicates the rhythm but maintains a separate contour. Throughout, it is assigned chord tones to provide consonance with the melody. Countermelody independence is increased by the use of a separate text in the first phrase, which is derived from a well-known carol. Unity is achieved through the recurrence of the word "alleluia" and the dotted rhythmic pattern in both parts. The accompaniment adds harmonic support while duplicating the melody in the first soprano.

The baritone is assigned the original melody in Example 9–7, while the soprano and alto are paired with a countermelody. These upper two parts are essentially written in a note-against-note setting using longer note values which complement the original melody. Key words or phrases from the original melody are assigned to the countermelody. The soprano and alto parts use primarily consonant chord tones. The accompaniment again adds chordal support, with occasional rhythmic figures to fill in the longer rhythmic values in the voice parts.

Example 9–5. Traditional (arr. H. Wilson and W. Ehret): *Winds through the Olive Trees*

Harry Wilson and Walter Ehret, *Prentice-Hall Choral Series*, Book 2, Englewood Cliffs, NJ, 1960. Used by permission.

Example 9–6. Traditional (arr. J. North): *Sing Noel and Beat the Drum*

Example 9–7. Mallet (arr. D. Riley and D. Wilson): *Garden Song*

© 1980 Cherry Lane Music Co. Reprinted with permission.

Figuration

Figurations are noncontinuous, fragmentary lines that add rhythmic and melodic punctuation to the original melody. In three-part textures, the figuration often occurs in two voices paired in a note-against-note texture entering at points where there is little or no motion in the original melody. Figurations employ text fragments which relate to the original text.

The second soprano and alto combine in Example 9–8 to form the figuration. The text fragment from the beginning of the first soprano part is repeated with each statement of the figuration. Note that even in this texture the traditional SSA close voicing is maintained.

Example 9–9 presents a similar handling of a figuration pattern, except that the nonadjacent soprano and baritone are combined for the "hallelu" figuration. One of the reasons for this combination is that the arranger intends the middle part to be sung by cambiata voices. The limited range, rhythmic treatment, and easily remembered melody present typical characteristics for this voice classification. Here the accompaniment helps to fill out the harmony for the figuration, while in Example 9–8, the accompaniment supported the melody line, leaving the figuration independent. Both cases exemplify the non-continuous, fragmentary characteristics of figuration.

Example 9–8. Traditional (arr. E. Lojewski): *Just a Closer Walk with Thee*

Ostinato

An ostinato is a one- or two-measure repeated motive that reiterates a single line of text. As in other applications of counterpoint to three-part textures, two voice parts are normally combined in a note-against-note setting of either the melody or the ostinato and the remaining voice part is assigned whichever part the paired voices do not sing. Depending on the harmony implied by the original melody, the ostinato may either stay at the same pitch level or vary pitch levels.

The two-measure ostinato in Example 9–10 is established in the introduction before the main melody enters at measure 5 below the ostinato. The ostinato is in a parallel third, note-against-note setting in the soprano and alto, and uses the "doodle-oo-doo" text. The melodic material for the ostinato is derived from the beginning of the melody, providing an obvious unifying link between the ostinato and the melody. The pitch level of the ostinato changes in measures 7 and 9 as the harmony implied by the melody changes. The accompaniment is independent of either the ostinato or the melody, providing chordal support and reiterating the dotted rhythmic pattern characteristic of both the ostinato and the melody.

Example 9–9. L. Bricusse and A. Newley (arr. R. Carlyle): *Gonna Build a Mountain*

From the Musical Production *Stop the World—I Want to Get Off*, words and music by Leslie Bricusse and Anthony Newley. © 1961 TRO Essex Music Ltd., London, England. TRO–Ludlow Music, Inc., New York. Used by permission. Complete arrangements in this series are available from TRO–Songways Service, Inc., 170 N.E. 33rd St., Ft. Lauderdale, Florida 33334.

Imitation

New lines of text or new sections of a choral arrangement are often set off by imitation. The pitch levels of the imitation are influenced by the total range possibilities of the three parts. For the range limitation of SSA, unison imitation is frequently found. Also possible is a second entry at the perfect fifth or fourth and a third entry at the octave. This latter possibility also exists in SAB settings, as well as simple imitation at the octave. In either SSA or SAB, typical voice-order entry patterns are either high-middle-low or low-middle-high. The controlling factors in deciding the level of imitation are the overall range of voices involved in the imitation, the voice order, and the range of the short idea receiving imitative treatment.

The imitation in Example 9–11 occurs near the end of the arrangement and contrasts this setting of the refrain with earlier unison and homophonic settings. The basic melodic idea is one and a half measures long and is imitated at the unison. The third entry in the alto is actually an incomplete entry of the melodic idea. This imitation at the unison is an obvious choice with the SSA voicing, the key of the arrangement, and the range of the melodic idea. After all three voices have entered, the texture becomes homophonic.

For a more detailed discussion of imitation at the fifth or fourth for SAB settings, the reader is directed to the section on imitation found in Chapter 10.

MODEL ARRANGEMENT

Goin' to Boston (arr. H. Wilson and W. Ehret) Music contained in Appendix II.

The basic form for each verse of this folk song is AAB, with each section eight measures long. The gender implications of the text help to determine the form of the three verses. The overall structure of the arrangement is as follows:

ARRANGEMENT FORM	Intro	A	A	B	Interlude	A	A	B	Interlude	A	A	B	Ending
TOTAL MEASURES	10	8	8	8	4+4	8	8	8	4+4	8	8	8	6
REHEARSAL NUMBERS ON SCORE	Beginning	2	3	4	5		2	3	4	5		6	7	8

The following textures are found in this arrangement:

Rehearsal 1: Imitation (at the unison)
Rehearsal 2: Unison

Example 9–10. B. G. De Sylva, L. Brown, and R. Henderson (arr. D. Besig): *Button Up Your Overcoat*

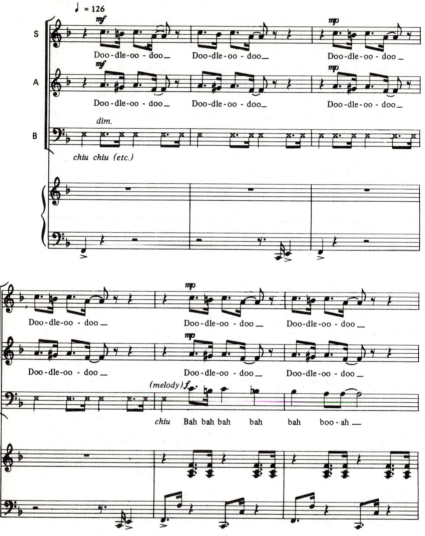

Reprinted by permission of Hal Leonard Publishing Corporation.

Example 9–11. Traditional (arr. W. Williamson): *Joshua Fit the Battle of Jericho*

Rehearsal 3:   Note-against-note (two part)

Rehearsal 4:   SA note-against-note with melody
              B ostinato

Rehearsal 5:   Note-against-note (two part sustained)

Rehearsal 6:   SA in note-against-note ostinato
              B melody

Rehearsal 7:   S melody
              A figuration
              B ostinato
              All parts interchange every two measures

Rehearsal 8:   SA note-against-note with melody
              B ostinato

Ending: Note-against-note

ARRANGING EXERCISES

1. Arrange *Magic Penny* for SAB, placing the melody in the soprano part, with a background vocal texture for alto and baritone. Starting in measure 9, begin a note-against-note texture. For the final eight measures use a counter-melody in the baritone against the soprano and alto note-against-note texture.

2. Write an SSA setting of *Johnny Has Gone for a Soldier*. Compose a countermelody for first soprano and set the second soprano and alto in note-against-note texture to include the melody. Write a freely composed introduction for this song using imitation in all three voices.

3. Practice composing a longer figuration in a setting of the spiritual *Were You There?* for SSA. A text fragment that comprises a complete thought should be used with the figuration. Assign the figuration pattern to the alto and a note-against-note texture with the melody to the two soprano parts. Change the texture in the last eight measures to note-against-note in all parts.

4. Compose a baritone ostinato to be used in counterpoint against a note-against-note setting of the folk melody *My Horses Ain't Hungry* in soprano and alto. Use a text fragment that fits in with the original text. Change to a different SAB texture for the last ten measures.

CHAPTER TEN

FOUR-PART ARRANGING

THE FOUR-PART ARRANGEMENT UTILIZES A FULL COMPLEMENT of choral resources, resulting in a rich sound characterized by harmonic completeness and contrapuntal complexity. Since four voices allow most harmonic configurations to be fully stated, the accompaniment is not needed to fulfill this role, and unaccompanied (*a cappella*) textures appear more frequently. The four-part *a cappella* choral sound presents one of the most expressive vocal combinations for nuance and vivid interpretation of the text. Examples in this chapter are chosen from both the accompanied and the *a cappella* literature, although common arranging techniques unite both approaches to four-part vocal writing. Of course, sections of a four-part arrangement will contain unison, two- and three-voice combinations; devices discussed in previous chapters devoted to these voice combinations would apply in these sections.

TYPICAL VOICE COMBINATIONS
AND APPLICATIONS

Most four-part arrangements are scored for the SATB voice combination, the main focus of this chapter. With mature singers, these four voices provide the arranger with at least a three-octave vocal range wherein a wide variety of textures and chord voicings can be effectively utilized.

Other typical four-part voice combinations include the all-male TTBB and the all-female SSAA. All textures described in this chapter apply to these two combinations as readily as they do the SATB. The TTBB grouping is particularly expressive in unaccompanied arranging, since the male voice is both resonant and rich in overtones. As explained in the discussion of three-part arranging (Chapter 9), the relatively high tessitura of the SSAA grouping often leads the arranger to provide an accompaniment to strengthen the fundamental bass of the harmony. "Barbershop" arranging presents special technical features and will be discussed in the section on all-female and all-male arranging at the end of this chapter.

HOMOPHONIC TEXTURES

Note-against-Note

The note-against-note texture is often used for short sections of choral arrangements where the melodic line has fairly fluid rhythmic motion. It is particularly useful in emphasizing text, since all voice parts articulate the text simultaneously using the rhythmic pattern of the melody. The melody is always assigned to the soprano or top voice; the lowest part most often contains the fundamental bass for the harmony, especially in *a cappella* arrangements.

Example 10–1 illustrates this texture in a sacred *a cappella* setting of *He Is*

Example 10–1. Traditional (arr. R. Wagner): *He Is Born*

Example 10–2. Schmidt (arr. R. Noeltner): *Soon It's Gonna Rain*

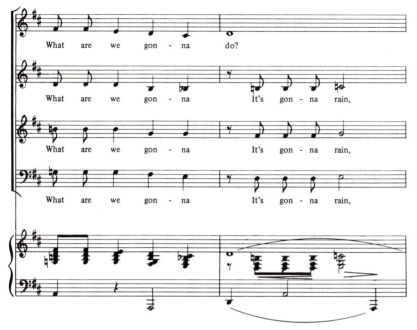

Born. Note the variety of open and close voicings used in the example, as well as the parallel and, especially, contrary voice motion. The wide range of the SATB combination allows this flexible approach to both chord voicings and motion.

The setting of *Soon It's Gonna Rain* in Example 10–2 also uses a variety of chord voicings and motion. But here, the subphrases in measures 1 and 3 proceed in open voicing and parallel motion, only to cadence in contrary motion and close voicing at the end of measures 2 and 4. Normally, parallel writing style would only proceed for a very few chords before need for variety and range restrictions necessitate a change to contrary motion. Example 10–2 also illustrates how an accompaniment can complement note-against-note choral textures, filling out the harmonies and providing rhythmic motion when notes of longer duration occur in the choral parts.

Animated Homophony

The animated homophonic texture rhythmically elaborates the note-against-note texture, keeping the melody in the soprano part and articulating the same line of text in all parts simultaneously. It is often used as a textural variant after a clear and simpler original presentation of the melody. Any one or two of the lower voices add additional embellishing tones to the note-against-note setting. These embel-

Example 10–3a. Traditional: *How Many Roads* (note-against-note)

lishing tones usually move in step motion, sometimes moving in give-and-take from one voice to the next, and sometimes pairing two voices together in parallel thirds, sixths, or tenths. Typical of this style is a continuous eighth-note motion between the embellishing activity in the lower voices and the melody in the soprano line.

Examples 10–3a and b illustrate this procedure. A basic four-part harmonization of the folk song *How Many Roads* in note-against-note style appears in Example 10–3a. This harmonically simple version should be completed to establish basic voice leading and distribute chord tones appropriately among the parts before moving to the animated version that follows in Example 10–3b. Two types of eighth-note activity are common. One of these is exemplified in measure 1 of the latter example, where the eighth-note motion embellishes the tonic triad. The other type occurs in measure 6 (bass part), where the eighth-note motion connects one chord to another. (An upper neighbor embellishment is added at the beginning.) Once the basic motion is planned, another voice can often be paired in parallel thirds or sixths, as seen in several locations in the example. An important musical aim is to balance the eighth-note motion among parts as much as possible.

The folk-tune setting in Example 10–4 also illustrates this technique. There is continuous eighth-note movement throughout that is emphasized by the staggered entrances in the first and third measures. Note also the parallel thirds between the lower voices in measure 2, and between tenor and bass in measure 5. There is a preponderance of step connection in the lower voices' eighth-note motion—particularly the long descending step line resulting from the staggered entrances in measures 3 and 4 and the tenor-bass pairing in measure 5.

Example 10–3b. Traditional: *How Many Roads* (animated homophony)

Example 10–4. Traditional (arr. L. Stone): *Black Is the Color of My True Love's Hair*

Melody Line with Background
Vocal Texture

Another useful homophonic texture for the initial presentation of a melody or for short sections of textural contrast is the melody line with background vocal support. The melody can occur in any voice part, although the outer voices (soprano or bass) are most frequently chosen. The other voices are then combined in a note-against-note homophonic texture that moves in longer rhythmic values than the melody. Either neutral syllables or single words relating to the text of the melody are assigned the background voices. These parts are designed to be simple lines which are subordinated to the melodic line, yet still have intrinsic melodic interest.

In Example 10–5, the melody occurs in the soprano, while the other parts provide harmonic support. For the most part, the support voices articulate words of text on downbeats at the same time as the soprano. Although in this way the supporting voices emphasize key words of text, which do not necessarily make up a complete thought, the arranger should be encouraged to group such words into a complete thought to help achieve linear integrity.

The supporting voices in Example 10–6 show a bit more independence. Supporting the tenor melody is a barbershop-style pattern in which the bass provides the harmonic support in long rhythmic values and the soprano and alto couple in offbeat chords which are harmonically completed in the accompaniment. Even though these supporting voices are assigned the neutral syllable "hm," care must be taken in performance to assure that such an active background part does not compete with the melody.

CONTRAPUNTAL TEXTURES

Countermelody

Countermelody does not occur as frequently in four-part textures as it does in two- or three-part textures. In SATB arranging, the countermelody is normally added during the last verse or at the conclusion of an arrangement to help achieve a climax. The independent line is most frequently found in a separate soprano part that sounds above the primary soprano part assigned the melody; the melody is supported by a note-against-note setting in the three lower parts. The arrangement, therefore, is actually a five-part setting. Typical performance practice is to assign a few very high sopranos to the countermelody, with the rest assigned to the melody. In SATB arrangements, unlike two- or three-part arrangements, the countermelody does not usually occur in a lower part below the melody. Either a neutral vowel sound or a text derived from, or related to, the original text is assigned to the countermelody.

The countermelody in Example 10–7 uses a variety of rhythmic values that complement the melody, utilizing the text of the original melody but displacing it by one measure. This line is composed of chord tones (and a few passing tones)

Example 10–5. Traditional (arr. M. Vance): *Pretty Saro*

Example 10–6. Daniels (arr. H. Wilson and W. Ehret): *You Tell Me Your Dream*

Harry Wilson and Walter Ehret, *Prentice-Hall Choral Series*, Book 3, Englewood Cliffs, NJ, 1960. Reprinted by permission.

Example 10–7. Williams: *Praise the Lord, Ye Heavens, Adore Him*

Example 10–8. Traditional (arr. W. Ehret): *Sinner Man*

consonant with the lower parts. The melody for this hymn tune occurs in the primary soprano part, while the lower three parts are primarily in a note-against-note texture with the melody.

Figuration

Figurations are non-continuous, fragmentary lines that provide rhythmic and melodic punctuation to the original melody. In four-voice textures, figurations occur in note-against-note texture in three voices, with the melody in the remaining voice (usually soprano or bass). The figurations enter at points where there is little or no rhythmic motion in the melody, employing text fragments which relate to the original text. In Example 10–8, the melody is assigned to the bass voice. Every two measures a figuration occurs in the upper three voices, joined in note-against-note texture, using the text fragment that immediately preceded it in the bass. In this way, the figuration reemphasizes the main phrases of text. It also provides rhythmic continuity, with the offbeat beginnings following immediately after the articulation of the longer rhythmic values in the melody. These offbeat punctuations are reinforced by the chordal treatment in the piano.

The figuration treatment in Example 10–9 contrasts with the previous example. The gospel-style arrangement is set up as a solo with SATB accompaniment. The figurations in measure 4 are essentially in unison. Then an alternation begins between figurations (measures 6 and 8) and background harmony (measure 7). This adaptation allows greater continuity in the choral parts. The spirit of the figuration is maintained by using the neutral syllable ''oo'' when the solo voice is active, and text fragments from the beginning of the verse for all the punctuations during the rhythmic lulls in the melodic line. The syncopated chordal accompaniment helps to establish the free, gospel style of the arrangement.

Ostinato

An ostinato is a short repeated motive which reiterates a single line of text. In four-part textures, one voice is usually assigned the melody, while the other voices combine in either note-against-note or contrapuntal texture with the ostinato. The ostinato may either stay at the same pitch level or vary pitch levels, depending on the harmony implied by the original melody. Ostinatos are effective in passages where the melody has little harmonic change at the beginning.

The ostinato of Example 10–10 is a one-measure idea in the tenor and bass that was stated by itself as a brief introduction earlier in this section of the arrangement. The pitch material is comprised of a *c* pedal in the bass and a *g–a* alternation in the tenor, reflecting the tonic implication of the melody. Only one word of text relating to the ''old ship of Zion'' is chosen for the ostinato. In measure 6, a third component of the ostinato is added in the soprano part. Although this line couples rhythmically with the tenor, it is a two-measure idea. The added soprano line helps to provide interest to the basic ostinato, which becomes tedious in a short time.

Example 10–11 shows a one-measure idea in the three upper parts that outlines a tonic seventh chord. The texture here attempts to imitate a plucked guitar, distributing the notes of the ostinato among the upper voices. The lack of harmonic change in the ostinato until measure 5 reflects a similar lack in the melody.

Imitation

Sections of imitative texture in choral arrangements are shorter and more limited than in the typical contrapuntal composition. Imitation is usually applied only to section beginnings to bring attention to a short melodic motive and a line of text. As soon as the imitation is completed, the texture usually becomes homophonic. The melodic material which accompanies the second and third imitative entries tends to be very simple harmonic support rather than elaborate contrapuntal lines

Example 10–9. Traditional (arr. P. Sjolund): *Go Tell It on the Mountain*

Example 10–10. Traditional (arr. R. H. Smith): *The Old Ship of Zion*

which compete with the main idea. Imitative section beginnings may occur in introductions, endings, or at section beginnings near the end of the arrangement to provide contrast and help achieve climax in the arrangement.

Since imitation frequently proceeds from lower to higher adjacent voices in choral arrangements, it often occurs at the fifth and fourth above to allow the idea to be presented in a comfortable range in all voice parts. Another consideration in selecting the interval of imitation is the pitch level desired for the final entry. Most imitative sections use the opening motive of a complete melodic idea as the basis of the imitation. The last voice to enter normally continues to present the entire melodic idea in the tonic key. Therefore, the previous pitch levels must be selected in such a way as to lead logically to the final entry in the tonic key. For this reason, three voices frequently participate in imitation in SATB texture, with the tonal order tonic-dominant-tonic (fifth and then fourth above). If four voices participate in the imitation, the order might be dominant-tonic-dominant-tonic (fourth, fifth, and then fourth above) to allow the final entry in tonic. Consider Example 10–12, an imitative section beginning for the folk song *Jennie Jenkins*.

The example is written to show a possible imitative beginning for the last verse of the folk song. In the first step, a motif that presents an initial musical and textual thought is derived from the first phrase of music. In this example, the four-note motive is two measures long. The second step is to decide on the number of voices participating in the imitation, and the pitch level of the final entry. Here the soprano

Example 10–11. Traditional (arr. L. Kjielson): *I'm Just a Poor Wayfarin' Stranger*

Example 10–12. Traditional: *Jennie Jenkins*

voice has the final entry and continues from this entry to complete the first phrase of the verse in the tonic key. With four voices participating in the imitation, the voice order becomes dominant-tonic-dominant-tonic. If only three voices had participated in the imitation, the first entry would have been on the tonic (as in measure 3). In such a situation, either the tenor or bass alone, or both men's parts combined, could have been assigned the first entry.

The third step is to write harmonic support parts for voices which have already entered. In Example 10–12, simple chordal support with the neutral syllable ''mm'' is constructed so as to offer little competition with the imitative entries. After all voices have entered with the imitative motive, the arrangement continues in a homophonic style with the melody in the soprano.

Example 10–13 provides an illustration of imitation as an introduction to the setting of the spiritual *Ain't That Good News*. The arranger initially selected, as the basis for the motivic imitation, a four-note motive which was associated with the presentation of the main line of text throughout the arrangement. Secondly, the arranger decided that the voice order would proceed from low to high and involve all four voices. The pitch levels of imitation are not as clearly predetermined as in the previous example, simply because the soprano or last entry voice does not necessarily have to continue with a melodic line in an introduction. In this example, the arranger selected tonic-dominant-tonic-mediant pitch relationships. He could have selected the dominant for the final entry, but since the harmonic support plan is to sustain the entry note, an incomplete triad (with no third) would then have resulted. Hence, the mediant entry is selected for the soprano to fill out the third of the tonic triad and to lead logically into the next subphrase which completes the introduction. Note how the arranger leads directly into note-against-note writing in the second phrase of text once the soprano voice has completed the final imitative entry.

Example 10–13. Traditional (arr. H. Wilson and W. Ehret): *Ain't That Good News?*

Harry Wilson and Walter Ehret, *Prentice-Hall Choral Series*, Book 3, Englewood Cliffs, NJ, 1960. Reprinted by permission.

SPECIAL FEATURES CONCERNING
ALL-FEMALE AND ALL-MALE ARRANGEMENTS

All-Female Arrangements

The most common treble-voice combinations are SA, SSA, and SSAA. Arranging concepts which relate to the SA combination are discussed in Chapter 5. The SSA combination, which occurs very frequently, is discussed in some detail in Chapter 9 ("Three-Part Arranging"). The least common combination, SSAA, shows many of the same limitations outlined in the SSA discussion. The primary restriction for SSAA arranging is the range: $(f)g–g^2(a^2)$. Complete harmonic structures can be voiced within these two octaves, but the tessitura is high for the fundamental bass in the alto to provide the full harmonic support that is available when male voices sound a full octave lower. For this reason, many SSA and SSAA arrangements are accompanied, allowing the lowest voice part to either double the fundamental bass part or provide another note in the harmony.

The melody is usually found in the highest soprano part. Homophonic textures (particularly note-against-note) predominate, with occasional use of contrapuntal texture for contrast. Effective short sections with the melody assigned to the lowest alto part also help to provide contrast. The general guideline is to assign melodies to outer voices (but to the second soprano in the "Sweet Adeline" style as explained in the barbershop section of this chapter). Chord voicing and connection are also affected by the SSAA range restriction, resulting in frequent closely-voiced chords and parallel motion between chords.

Many of these features can be seen in the *a cappella* setting of *Carol of the Birds* in Example 10–14. In the first four measures, the melody is found in the combined alto parts or the lowest alto part (measures 3 and 4); while in the last four measures, the melody is sung by the first soprano. Homophonic texture occurs throughout. Note also the close voicing and parallel chord motion (measures 2, 4, 6, and 8), which are so characteristic of the all-female chorus.

The accompanied SSAA setting in Example 10–15 also illustrates close chord voicing in the choral parts. The accompaniment doubles most of these notes, but expands the voicings so that the fundamental bass part is in a lower octave than the second alto part, and also adds a countermelody above the notes of the first soprano to help achieve a triumphant climax to the chorus.

All-Male Arrangements

Most all-male arrangements are for TTBB, with only occasional TBB or TB settings. One of the main reasons for the great amount of all-male literature is the history of all-male singing, which incorporates such diverse groups as British singing societies, military choruses, glee clubs in men's colleges, and barbershop quartets. Today many of these groups do not function in the same way they once did because of the changing roles of men and women in society. But since these male singing groups did flourish earlier in this century, a large body of literature was written and arranged to fill the demand.

Example 10–14. Traditional (arr. D. Malin): *Carol of the Birds*

Example 10–15. Traditional (arr. R. Elmore and R. Reed): *Long Years Ago in Bethlehem*

Rich in resonance and overtones, male voices are frequently arranged *a cappella*. Although the male range $(F)G–g^1(a^1)$ has the same general two-octave restriction as female range, the tessitura is one octave lower, allowing the fundamental bass part to sound in the range where it fully supports the harmonic structure. As in all-female arrangements, melodies frequently occur in the top part; but unlike the all-female arrangement, melodies are also frequently assigned to the interior second tenor or baritone parts. In many arrangements, the melody will move from part to part, even within a phrase, as the melodic range moves from higher to lower or vice versa. Homophonic textures (particularly note-against-note) predominate, with occasional use of counterpoint. Close chord voicings with both parallel and contrary motion between chords are found. Particular care is needed in a close voicing low in the male tessitura to avoid a thick, muddy sound. A convenient rule of thumb is that no interval smaller than a fifth should be used between two pitches which are both below $e\flat$.

Example 10–16 shows two characteristic male homophonic textures (note-against-note and background homophonic texture) with the melody in the first tenor. Observe that the second tenor momentarily goes above the first tenor melody at the cadence in measure 4 to preserve voice leading and maintain closely voiced chords that are not too low in the tessitura. Note also the preponderance of closely voiced chords with both parallel and contrary motion.

The setting of *Great Is Thy Faithfulness* in Example 10–17 illustrates the shift of melody from first tenor to baritone within one section. The reason for the shift is that the tessitura of the first phrase of the melody is relatively high, whereas in the second phrase it is in a middle range. If the melody were retained in the first tenor for the second phrase and the other voices remained below it, a very dense, muddy, and poorly voiced section would result. The change of voicing is enhanced by a change from note-against-note to background homophonic texture, thus allowing the melody to prevail.

Barbershop Quartets and Sweet Adelines

Barbershop arranging is a particular style of all-male arranging that deserves special mention. Fortunately, through the national S.P.E.B.S.Q.S.A. (the Society for the Preservation and Encouragement of Barber Shop Quartet Singing in America), barbershop quartet singing has flourished throughout the United States for many years. The female counterparts to barbershop singers are referred to as "Sweet Adelines." Although originally intended for one-on-a-part singing, arrangements in this style are also performed by all-male or all-female choruses, but always *a cappella*.

The basic arranging texture in this style is note-against-note, with the melody always remaining in the second tenor (or second soprano) part. The melody part is referred to as the *lead*, and the rules of the S.P.E.B.S.Q.S.A. forbid either the top part or the lower parts to carry the melody. The top part (first tenor or first soprano) remains above the lead throughout, singing a part comprised of chord tones basically consonant with the lead. The third part (baritone or first alto) also provides a part which harmonizes with the lead, although this part is permitted to cross above the lead for voice-leading purposes. The lowest part (bass or second alto) provides the supporting bass line for the harmony, since there is no accompaniment to fulfill this function.

Rich harmonies colored with chromatic chords are an important part of the style. Unexpected chord resolutions and unusual voice leading are used to achieve the greatest harmonic interest.

Two additional factors in barbershop style are *slides* and *tags*. *Slides* occur when the lead sustains a melody note (usually at phrase cadences) while the other three parts move in faster rhythmic values in three-voice note-against-note texture.

Example 10–16. Traditional (arr. A. Parker and R. Shaw): *O Tannenbaum*

© 1953 G. Schirmer, Inc. Reprinted with permission.

The *tag* is the special ending for the arrangement where particularly chromatic and unusual chords are used.

Example 10–18 provides a complete barbershop arrangement of *My Wild Irish Rose*. Note how the melody is in the second tenor, while the first tenor remains above it. On the other hand, the baritone part frequently crosses the second tenor, as in measures 8–12. Slides occur at almost every cadence point, as in measures 7–8, 15–16, and 19–20. The tag in this arrangement repeats the last four measures of the tune with the same basic harmony plus the slide in the last two measures.

Example 10–17. W. Runyan (arr. M. Hayes): *Great Is Thy Faithfulness*

Example 10–18. C. Olcott (arr. F. Connett): *My Wild Irish Rose*

© 1984 Don Gray (SPEBSQSA). Used by permission.

MODEL ARRANGEMENT

Swansea Town (arr. G. Holst)

Each verse of this folksong is sixteen measures long, followed by an eight-measure chorus. There are four verses in Holst's *a cappella* arrangement.

ARRANGEMENT FORM	Verse 1	Chorus	Verse 2	Chorus	Interlude	Verse 3	Verse 4	Chorus
TOTAL MEASURES	16	8	16	8	1	17	16	8
MEASURE NUMBERS ON SCORE	1–16	17–24	25–40	41–48	49	50–66	67–82	83–90

The following textures are found in this arrangement:

m. 1–15:   Unison (TB)
 m. 16:   Imitation
m. 17–20:   Countermelody (melody in B)
m. 21–24:   Unison and note-against-note
m. 25–39:   Note-against-note
 m. 40:   Imitation
m. 41–44:   Countermelody (melody in B)
m. 45–48:   Unison and note-against-note
m. 48–66:   Melody with ostinato
m. 67–86:   Countermelody (melody in B)
m. 87–90:   Unison and note-against-note (brief imitation)

ARRANGING EXERCISES

1. Arrange *Gypsy Rover* for SATB, placing the melody in the soprano part, with a background vocal texture for alto, tenor, and bass. Each part should have linear and textual integrity. Starting in measure 7, begin a note-against-note texture.

2. Write a harmonically simple note-against-note setting of *I Know Where I'm Going* for SATB. Using that setting as a basis, write an animated homophonic setting, with constant eighth-note motion.

3. Arrange the first eight measures of the spiritual *This Little Light of Mine* for TTBB in a barbershop setting. Add slides at appropriate cadence points.

4. Compose an imitative introduction to *Oh, Sinner Man* using all four SATB voices. Use a two-measure motive derived from the melody as the basis for the imitation. Set one verse of this folk song using a two-voice ostinato accompaniment. Place the melody in a combined men's or women's part.

CHAPTER ELEVEN

SPECIAL
CHORAL DEVICES

AN ARRANGEMENT CAN BE GREATLY ENHANCED by calling upon choral devices—
sonorities and techniques—that are not specifically in the source material but add
variety and color, and sometimes provide a special focus for certain elements of
the text.

SPECIAL SONORITIES

The chorus can be used in several creative ways besides text singing. The following
are some of the common approaches used to create special sonorities with voices.

Neutral Syllables

The most common use of the chorus in the realm of special sonorities is as
background for the melody. One or more of the parts can sing neutral syllables to
provide harmony or motion without interfering with the melody. "Mm" (or "hmm")
is the quietest neutral syllable; "ooh" (or "oo") is more haunting or fluid; "ah"
projects the most and can give strong thrust to a passage.

Neutral syllables are almost indispensable for *a cappella* arranging, providing
needed contrast to the text and creating a foreground-background texture. They can
also be used in an introduction (even when a piano accompanies) to involve the
chorus without anticipating the text. In Example 11–1, note the use of the more
dramatic "ah" for the introduction, followed by "oo" to prepare and then support
the melody.

Example 11–1. Grier (arr. G. Grier and L. Everson): *Life Is a Dream*

Imitating Specific Instruments or Sounds

The chorus can make the sounds of instruments—cymbals, tuba, trumpet, and so on—that are closely associated with a style or text. As shown in Example 11–2, this can immediately define the arrangement's style, while bringing freshness to the choral role.

Example 11–2. Sylvia, Brown, and Henderson (arr. D. Besig): *Button Up Your Overcoat*

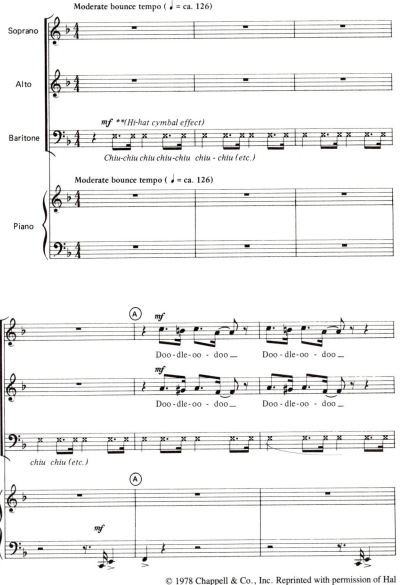

An entire section might be devoted to such instrumental sounds as long as the material is related to the text in an important way. For example, it seems natural that *Hey, Mr. Banjo* would give a "solo" to the banjo-turned-chorus. In Example 11–3, both "text" and musical style contribute to the idiom.

Example 11–3. Morgan and Malkin (arr. C. Cassey): *Hey, Mr. Banjo*

A most sophisticated and effective use of imitative sound in the text is shown in Example 11–4. The churning of Ezekiel's wheel is captured in a complex layering of individually simple and repetitive parts.

Scat Singing

A great deal of the early jazz instrumental music attempted to emulate the articulations, inflections, and embellishments of early blues singers. Later, many vocalists copied the angular and multi-timbred melodic lines of be-bop instrumentalists, improvising words and a wide range of syllabic utterances to capture the emotion of the song in a more abstract and varied manner than the regular text would permit. This latter vocal technique is referred to as *scat singing*. It is commonly used in vocal jazz arrangements today, whether improvised by a soloist (adhering to the harmonic progressions of the song) or written out by the arranger for part or all of the chorus to sing.

In Example 11–5a, scat syllables are sung by the choir, with parts entering one or two at a time to build excitement. Lines maintain their individuality through variety of articulation and timbre. Each line is easy to sing even at a fast tempo.

Example 11–4. Traditional (arr. W. Dawson): *Ezekiel Saw de Wheel*

Repeat this section (8 measures)
four times in the following manner.

1st time: All tenors sing the 2nd tenor part in unison.
2nd time: Tenors sing their respective parts and continue repeating with sopranos.
3rd time: All sopranos sing the 2nd soprano part in unison.
4th time: Sopranos sing their respective parts to the end of the piece.

Example 11–5a. Cahn, Stordahl, and Weston (arr. K. Shaw): *Day by Day*

Later in the same arrangement, scat syllables are used in an energetic "shout" chorus—chordal, richly-voiced, and in a high tessitura (Ex. 11–5b).

As suggested above, scat singing calls upon a wide variety of syllables, from the soft ("da-ba-da") to the more strident ("sca-ba-dwee"), and from the short ("dop") to the long ("vweeee"). In general, lines in the upper register use more bright syllables ("skwee"), while those descending to the lower register tend to reinforce the motion by using darker syllables ("bow"). The arranger should become familiar with the scat singing of the great jazz vocalists, so that the choral writing in this style will sound natural, effective, and stylistic.

Speaking

One spoken word or a passage of speaking, sometimes referred to as *parlando*, can be very effective if the tempo is brisk enough so that the percussive attack of the words hides the inevitable variety of inflection among speakers. The passage

Example 11–5b. "Shout" chorus. Cahn, Stordahl, and Weston (arr. K. Shaw): *Day by Day*

du bi du wi — du dah,— Bop bop du bi du wi — du da — dot du dot du — da — bop bop du dot da —

should be brief unless other lines—spoken or sung—are layered over it. Spoken rhythms should be notated conventionally, except that note heads should be replaced by "x's," as illustrated in Example 11–6. The word "spoken" or "whispered" above the staff at the onset of the passage further clarifies the notation.

Example 11–6.

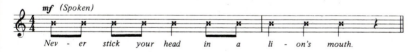

Nev - er stick your head in a li - on's mouth.

SPECIAL TECHNIQUES

Quite separate from the uses of the voice discussed above are writing devices that create their own special effect, yet do so through the conventional use of individual voices.

The Fan

The *fan*, so named because it resembles on paper the shape of a paper fan held sideways, begins the chorus on a unison pitch or closely voiced chord and expands outward—up in the women's parts and down in the men's parts. The resulting sense of burgeoning can be quite powerful.

A fan can be used when:

a. The melody naturally ascends with much stepwise motion (Ex. 11–7a).

b. The melody ascends by leap but, as it has been heard a few times previously in the arrangement, can be "filled in" to accomplish this effect (Ex. 11–7b).

c. The melody does not ascend but can be led into with newly composed material (Ex. 11–7c).

The first step in creating a fan is to determine the metric placement of the opening unison and the voicing of the chord of arrival. Then the connecting lines for each part can be written, keeping in mind that they should be fluid (essentially stepwise in relaxed rhythm) and directional, with outer voices eventually at least a third away from an inner voice, and implying conventional harmonies at certain points, but without real stability until the chord of arrival.

Example 11–7a. Duke Ellington: *In a Sentimental Mood*

© 1935 American Academy of Music, Inc. Reprinted with the permission of Belwin-Mills Publishing Corp.

Example 11–7b.

Example 11–7c.

Unconventional Harmonies

Example 11–8 is an illustration of linearly conceived harmony. Here the repeated ascending melody (*c* to *g*) and descending bass line (*c* down to *b*) provide an overall sense of direction for the passage. The alto and tenor parts contribute to the basically diatonic, tertian setting, but the sonorities which result from the confluence of the four lines within such a limited range (women rather low, men somewhat high) can be very dense and hauntingly beautiful. However, each line should be easy to sing, and the dense sonorities should be balanced (and kept fresh) by frequent use of unisons, open intervals, and triads.

Example 11–8.

A different harmonic approach is to build chords in fourths—either diatonic or perfect—from the melody (in the soprano part) down through the lowest voice. This can create complex and resonant sonorities, especially in an SATB setting, and can add a fresh sophistication to an arrangement. Since diatonic fourths are perfect or augmented, intervallic content changes from chord to chord (Ex. 11–9a), while chords built in perfect fourths move in exact parallel motion but include pitches not in the key (Ex. 11–9b). Because of its striking, but limited, nature, this device must not be overused.

Example 11–9a. Reharmonization of a melody in diatonic fourths.

Example 11–9b. Reharmonization of a melody with strictly parallel fourths.

The Pyramid

A common technique in big band writing, the pyramid layers pitches one on top of the other to create a dramatic ascent resulting in a dense sonority. At a fast tempo, pitches must not be too difficult for the singers to pre-hear, as the notes have to be ''picked out of the air'' (Ex. 11–10).

Example 11–10. Foster (arr. M. Hayes): *Some Folks*

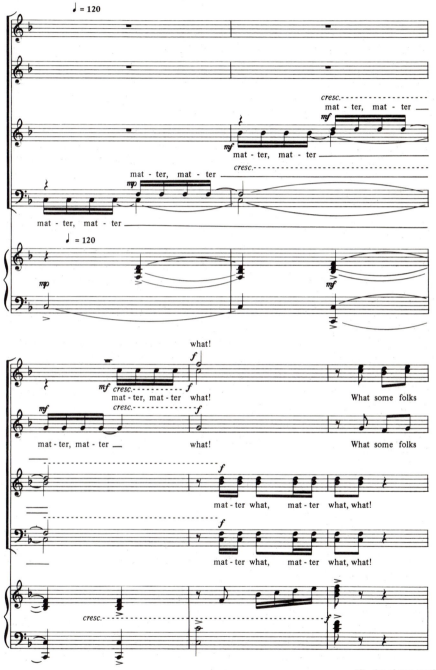

(Continued next page)

CHAPTER TWELVE

ADAPTING AN EXISTING ARRANGEMENT TO A DIFFERENT CHORAL COMBINATION

FREQUENTLY MORE THAN ONE SETTING OF A SINGLE basic choral arrangement is published to meet the varied ranges, maturity levels, and voice groupings of particular performing groups. Inevitably, this process involves a simple reworking of the musical materials to fit the ranges of the intended singers. This process can also be useful for the director who needs to adapt an existing arrangement to the voice combination of a particular ensemble.

ADAPTING THE SATB ARRANGEMENT

Although it is possible to adapt a choral arrangement written for any combination of voices to another combination, for purposes of illustration, this section focuses on adapting an SATB setting to four other common two- to four-voice combinations: SA, SAB, SSA, and TTBB. This adaptation provides a practical solution for the conductor faced with the necessity of adapting a superior SATB setting of a particular source to a less common voice combination. This discussion also serves to reinforce a number of musical principles which apply to particular voice combinations discussed in previous chapters of this book. Since most SATB arrangements involve four independent lines only for brief sections, rewriting an entire arrangement for fewer than four voices is not as big an undertaking as might be initially thought.

Original SATB Setting

The original SATB setting of *The Ash Grove*, which appears on the bottom four staves of Example 12–1, is a combination note-against-note and animated-homophonic treatment of the third verse of the folk song. Most eighth-note supporting motion appears in the alto and tenor parts, while the melody is in the soprano. The accompaniment is in a sustained chordal style that duplicates most of the notes found in the choral parts.

SA Setting

In the SA setting, the melody remains in the soprano part. The alto part combines portions of the original alto and tenor lines, retaining considerable eighth-note motion. The note choice for the alto part is governed by the desire to be consonant with the harmony of the accompaniment, while maintaining a predominance of thirds and sixths against the soprano on the beat, with occasional fourths and unisons.

SAB Setting

The SAB adaptation is obviously the closest to the original SATB, because both the soprano and baritone lines are retained exactly. The alto part is an amalgamation of the original alto and tenor lines, chosen to maintain as much eighth-note motion as possible as well as to combine with the soprano and baritone on the beat to form complete triads.

SSA Setting

The SSA setting retains the melody line in the first soprano part. The second soprano part retains most of the notes from the original alto part and the alto part uses some of the original tenor part, except where the range extends too low for the altos. The result is the typical close position voicing of the three parts, with the fundamental bass part in the piano accompaniment.

TTBB Setting

In TTBB arranging, the melody is usually assigned either to the first tenor or, in barbershop style, to the second tenor. In this illustration, the melody is found in the first tenor part to parallel the other settings which have the melody in the top part. Although the bass part shares many of the bass notes of the piano accompaniment, these notes are frequently an octave below the piano notes. For this reason, the piano part should add lower octaves in the TTBB setting to duplicate as much as possible the sounding octave of the bass part. Complete triads in close voicings occur except where the melody is so low (measures 4 and 6) that complete closely-voiced triads would be too muddy and therefore ineffective. Ideally, this setting would be transposed up at least a half step, because the bass is rather low and the first tenor could be higher. However, it is kept in the original key to facilitate comparisons with the other settings.

Example 12–1. Traditional (arr. L. Stone): *The Ash Grove*

ADAPTING HYMN SETTINGS

There are at least two ways that the church choir director can quickly adapt a four-voice hymn setting to provide variety in performance. In the first of these, the sopranos sing the alto part up an octave, as a descant, and the altos sing the soprano melody at the original pitch level. The second involves a TTBB performance of an SATB setting: the melody (original soprano line) is sung by the second tenor down an octave, barbershop style; the first tenor sings the original tenor part at the original pitch, the baritones sing the original alto down an octave, and the basses retain their original part. This allows all voice parts to sing in a comfortable range with the familiar barbershop sound characterized by close-voiced chords and second tenor melody. While this voice rearrangement works well with most hymns, there are occasionally problems when the baritones (singing the original alto part down an octave) actually go below the bass part, changing the chord inversion at that point.

Both the descant adaptation and the TTBB adaptation work effectively because hymn settings always involve simple triads or seventh chords with occasional non-chord tones on the offbeats that will have the same consonant sound regardless of the voice part assignment of particular triad members. Both these adaptations can be seen along with the original (lower two staves) SATB setting of the first line of the hymn tune *Hyfrydol* in Example 12–2.

Example 12–2. C. Wesley and R. Prichard: *Hyfrydol*

CHAPTER THIRTEEN

JAZZ
VOCAL STYLES

THE ABILITY TO WRITE IN SEVERAL STYLES is absolutely essential for the contemporary professional choral arranger. This is due to two factors: first, jazz, gospel, rock, country, and pop music are increasingly included in performances by school, church, and community choirs, and a great demand for well-arranged literature in these styles has resulted; second, just as European folk music had a dramatic influence on the art music of that continent, so American folk music is merging with traditional art music to form highly sophisticated and meaningful modes of expression. To create the appropriate traditional context of a given source—thus providing its emotional ''roots''—the arranger should be fully versed in the techniques which distinguish the various styles.

Jazz is the broadest and often the most sophisticated of these styles. This chapter focuses upon a contemporary jazz style that adapts well to the choir, while maintaining to a great degree the emotional intensity most often associated with the solo vocal performance.

RHYTHM

The roots of jazz are in both West African traditional music and Western European music of the eighteenth and nineteenth centuries. Broadly speaking, Western European music of that period relies heavily upon melodic subtlety and harmonic complexity for interest, while the emphasis in the music of West African cultures is on timbral subtlety and rhythmic complexity. Jazz borrows from the best of both traditions and is thus a unique idiom. Our discussion focuses upon each musical element individually, beginning with rhythm.

Jazz was synonymous with swing-style music until 1950, when other rhythmic styles began co-existing with swing. Nonetheless, swing is today a very important "feel" in jazz and has influenced all of the others that have become part of the jazz idiom.

Swing Notation

Because of its roots, swing cannot be written accurately using conventional (Western European) notation. The most accurate notation for a series of swing eighth notes would be:

Note that within a beat greater length (agogic accent) is given to the first note, but articulative stress is given to the second note. The latter's stress "pushes" the line into the next beat, thus creating the swing feel.

Note too that a series of such configurations makes the notation cumbersome to write and to read. As a result, vocal jazz arrangers have borrowed the instrumental notation practice of writing conventional eighth notes ♫ ♫ , and indicating at the beginning of the arrangement (next to the tempo indication) that the eighth notes are to be "swung." For performers familiar with the idiom, the indication "swing" or "swing feel" is sufficient. For less experienced performers, that indication plus the equation ♫ = ♩♪ is safest.

Sometimes the notation ♫.♫ is used. This is fine for young performers, who might have trouble conceptualizing the rhythmic transfer from notation to practice. However, it should not be used generally as it may lead to a stiff performance of the figure.

Syncopation

Rhythmic complexity can be created within a part or between parts. Within a part, the arranger should use some syncopation for vitality, but not so much that it becomes predictable or that the metric underpinning is lost. Example 13–1 transforms a source melody's quarter and half notes into a rhythmically interesting line. Note how this transformation maintains certain quarter notes so that the syncopation is fresh and effective, does not obscure text delivery, and includes rests so that the singers can breathe.

Later in the arrangement, where the tune is familiar and more activity is desired, greater use of syncopation may be appropriate. Metric disorientation may even be desirable for very brief passages in these later sections (Ex. 13–1c).

Example 13–1a. The source melody, Rodgers and Hart: *I Could Write a Book*

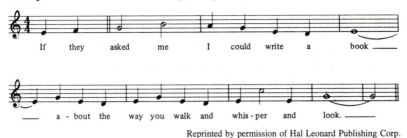

Reprinted by permission of Hal Leonard Publishing Corp.

Example 13–1b. Rhythmically transformed melody.

Example 13–1c. Greater rhythmic freedom.

This rhythmic fluidity and variety derive from individual styling and improvisation which are so much a part of jazz. The arranger is urged to create rhythmically exciting lines—particularly in homorhythmic passages—and to pace their complexity throughout the arrangement. Of course this should be balanced with the other elements: the more complex the rhythm of a given passage, the simpler the melodic, harmonic, and textural elements, and conversely.

Example 13–2. Fredrickson: *When I'm Near You*

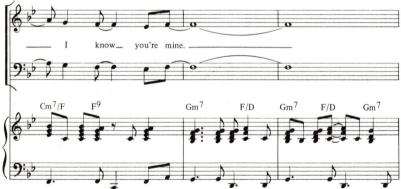

Even Eighth-Note Rhythm

Two jazz styles employing the conventional, even eighth-note rhythm will be discussed here. The first is the slow tune, referred to as the *ballad*, which employs traditional notation. The ballad is the closest rhythmically of the various jazz styles to its usual source, the show tune, although employing more rhythmic freedom and a small amount of syncopation.

The *bossa nova* (literally, "new beat") was brought to the United States from Latin America by jazz performers. The name itself calls attention to the style's rhythmic vitality. This is captured by the layering of several different rhythms played by accompanying instruments as discussed in Chapter 15. It is captured in the vocal parts by a good deal of gentle syncopation propelling a legato line, as illustrated in Example 13–2.

METER

Most swing tunes and ballads, and all bossa novas, are in $\frac{4}{4}$ meter; but instead of the metric weight falling on the first and third beats of the measure, the weight falls on the second and fourth beats. This is expressed primarily in the accompaniment (discussed in Chapter 15).

The jazz waltz, in $\frac{3}{4}$ meter, is different from other waltzes in underlying rhythmic and metric structure. The syncopation and varied articulation contribute to its propulsion, particularly at fast tempos (Ex. 13–3).

Example 13–3a. Conventional waltz rhythm.

Example 13–3b. Common jazz waltz rhythm.

Generally, the arrangement should assume the same meter as that of the source. However, it is not uncommon in the jazz idiom for a source in $\frac{4}{4}$ meter to be transfigured into a more "active" jazz waltz, or for an arrangement's first and last sections to be in $\frac{4}{4}$ while the middle section is in $\frac{3}{4}$.

Sometimes a source in $\frac{4}{4}$ will be arranged in an unusual meter such as $\frac{7}{8}$. This can be effective for a section of an arrangement, but the jolting reinterpretation of a standard tune can become overbearing if continued over a long period of time. The arranger must decide whether such metric manipulation is part of a natural evolution for the tune and arrangement.

TEMPO

Jazz performers are most familiar with tempo markings in the vernacular. Common markings are (from fast to slow):

Fast swing	Fast bossa	Ballad
Up swing		
Medium swing	Medium bossa	
Easy swing	Relaxed (slow) bossa	

Also common is the style indication plus a metronome marking:

Swing ($\quad$ = 144)   Bossa nova ($\quad$ = 120)

The tempo of a jazz arrangement generally should not change within a section, since the steadiness of pulse is so idiomatic and essential for syncopations and counter-rhythms to be perceived as such. Only a slow introduction, interlude, or ending section may be *rubato* or *ritardando* toward its end. If the arranger wishes to create a sense of slowing down in a swing arrangement, for example, the *ritardando* should be written out "in time," usually by doubling the rhythmic value of the notes in the final phrase (Ex. 13–4).

Example 13–4. Van Heusen: *Here's That Rainy Day*

    a. Source melody.

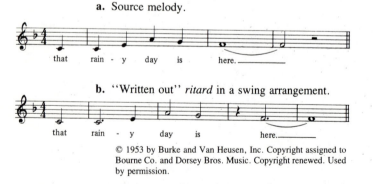

    b. "Written out" *ritard* in a swing arrangement.

© 1953 by Burke and Van Heusen, Inc. Copyright assigned to
Bourne Co. and Dorsey Bros. Music. Copyright renewed. Used
by permission.

Change of tempo *between* sections is quite common. After a slow introduction, the tempo of the "head" (section where the main melody is stated) is usually established before the main melody is stated.

In a ballad, it is effective to write the first section of the arrangement (possibly *a cappella*) quasi-*rubato*, and then write the second section in tempo. This may or may not be preceded by an introduction (Ex. 13–5).

Example 13–5. Van Heusen (arr. D. Riley and D. Wilson): *Darn That Dream*

A very simple, effective, and common way to suggest a change in tempo in the swing style is the move from a two-beat to a four-beat feel. At first two equal beats (half-note pulses) are perceived in each measure, but in later sections a four-beat pulse is established. This is achieved primarily in the accompaniment, and will be discussed in technical detail in Chapter 15. The arranger should be aware of the increased intensity achieved by "going into four" when planning an arrangement so that the change can be matched by appropriate vocal textures.

MELODIC INFLECTION

Jazz arrangements rely heavily upon the conventional major and minor modes, and, to a lesser degree, the dorian and mixolydian modes.

Out of the synthesis of European and African scales emerged the so-called *blues scale*. As with jazz rhythms, certain pitches of the blues scale cannot be notated using the conventional system. An approximation of the blues scale on C is illustrated in Example 13–6.

Example 13–6. Blues scale on C.

between E♭ & E♮

sometimes not considered part
of the blues scale on C

The problem of notation is compounded by the fact that most West African vocal music slides from pitch to pitch, constantly changing the timbre and articulation for expression. Therefore, the arranger must decide how much of the African (blues) side of jazz is to be expressed, and proceed to indicate, using conventional notation as a base, which "blue" notes, slides, and articulations should be used.

Notation of jazz pitch and articulation is gradually becoming standardized. Here is a list of the more common yet unconventional markings:[1]

   1. Vertical accent (ʌ) —normally occurs on the beat and is usually on a quarter note. The note is accented strongly, and held for less than its full value but longer than if staccato.

   2. Ascending glissando (♩↗↑)—an upward slide between two pitches.

   3. Descending glissando (↑↘♩)—a downward slide between pitches.

   4. Fall-off (♩↓) —a descending slide, usually followed by a rest; usually includes a decrescendo.

   5. Ascending smear (♩ or ♩)—a slide into a note from below; the pitch is reached just prior to the second note. One of the most common jazz inflections.

---

[1]This list is taken from Kirby Shaw's booklet, "Vocal Jazz Style" (Winona, MN: Hal Leonard Publishing Corporation, 1976), designed primarily as an aid for the performer.

6. Doit ⟨⟩ —an aggressive ascending slide which is followed by a rest; the inflected note is robbed of its pitch value.

7. Flip ⟨⟩—the sounding of the initial note and maintaining its pitch until just before the second note, whereupon there is a quick upward lift followed immediately by a rapid drop to the second note.

8. Shake ⟨⟩—the sounding of the inflected note, followed quickly by fairly fast and even movement between the written pitch and a pitch a major 2nd to perfect 4th above; the faster with tempo, the narrower the interval and faster the speed of the shake.

9. Ghost ⟨⟩ —a note needing a very soft but rhythmically vital sound.

10. Plop ⟨⟩ —the rapid sliding down to a given note from a large interval above; both pitches are accented, with the first occurring rhythmically as close as possible to the second.

These are demonstrated in Example 13–7. Of course the example is for illustration; the markings are too concentrated for an actual passage.

Example 13–7. Jazz pitch and articulation notation in context.

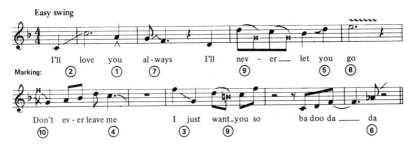

Many published arrangements do not include these indications, relying on the performers to stylize appropriately. It is best, however, for the arranger to communicate as completely, yet as clearly, as possible what pitch and articulation techniques are desirable. The swing feel is a certain approach to rhythm *in conjunction with* phrasing, pitch, and articulation.

HARMONY

Given the multi-colored palette of contemporary jazz vocabulary, the beginning arranger must be careful not to indulge in harmonic complexity for its own sake. Unison, two-part and triadic writing, and vocal rests are needed to balance texturally the complex sonorities that provide passages with special expressiveness. That said, the beauty and intricacy of many vocal jazz arrangements depend to a large degree on the use of chord extensions and substitutions, as well as on the specific arrangement of pitches within a chord, referred to as the *voicing*.

Chordal Extensions

As with music of the classical tradition, conventional jazz harmonies are constructed of chords built in thirds (Ex. 13–8).

Example 13–8.

Contemporary jazz styles are rarely restricted to triads, employing at least seventh chords consistently. In a major mode, diatonic seventh chords are constructed and identified as indicated in Example 13–9.

Example 13–9. Diatonic seventh chords.

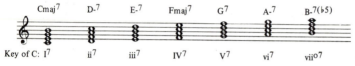

For more dense sonorities, 9ths can be added to seventh chords (Ex. 13–10). Note that the minor 9th interval occurs diatonically in the major mode in the iii^9 and $\overset{9}{vii}o7$ chords, and in the minor mode in the ii^9 and V^9. Alterations must be made in the first three, because only in the V^9 chord is the tension created by the minor 9th interval desirable.

Example 13–10. Ninth chords.

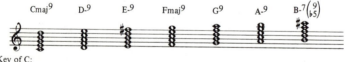

Similarly, an 11th can be added to all chords (Ex. 13–11). The diatonic 11th of IV is augmented; the 11ths of the two other major diatonic triads, I and V, are raised to become augmented in order to avoid the minor 9th interval between the 3rd and the 11th of the chord. (The raised 11th also reinforces the overtone relationship of those chords.)

Example 13–11. Eleventh chords.

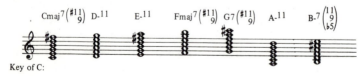

Also possible are 13th chords, which are frequently used without the inclusion of the 11th (Ex. 13–12). Note that when all of the pitches are arranged in stepwise fashion, they incorporate all of the notes of a diatonic scale. Any linear material sounding with a given chord, then, may be derived from this scale.

Example 13–12. Thirteenth chords.

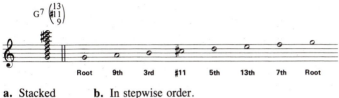

a. Stacked in thirds.   **b.** In stepwise order.

Obviously, using six or seven pitches in each voicing would be unmanageable. The following are voicing principles:

1. The third of the chord must be present to define the basic triadic quality.

2. The seventh should be present to define the seventh-chord quality.

3. The 11th may be supported, and the 13th is usually supported, by the 9th.

4. If tonal ambiguity is desired in a passage, exception may be made to 1, 2, and 3 above. The root may be omitted occasionally from even an *a cappella* passage, particularly if the harmonic function of the chord is clear from the progression.

Chord Alterations

1. The minor mode creates certain chords of different qualities from those of the major mode. Upper extensions intensify these differences (Ex. 13–13).

Example 13–13.

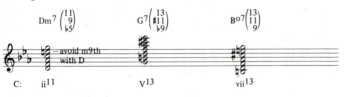

As in the classical tradition, these chords can be "borrowed" for use in the major mode when greater tension is desired. The net result is that the upper extensions of the chord as spelled in the original major mode appear to be altered (Ex. 13–14).

Example 13–14.

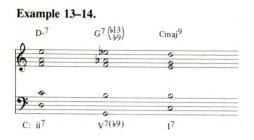

C: ii⁷   V⁷(♭9)   I⁷

2. The blues scale also affects harmonic structure. In fact, even diatonic seventh chords become significantly altered. However, while traditional blues melodies were very sophisticated, their harmonic structure evolved out of simple Protestant hymns and therefore relied heavily on I, IV, and V chords. These chords are usually notated as seventh chords in the manner illustrated in Example 13–15.

Example 13–15.

C blues: I⁷   IV⁷   V⁷

Evolving to 9th chords, the vocabulary becomes more complex (Ex. 13–16).

Example 13–16.

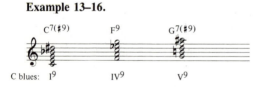

C blues: I⁹   IV⁹   V⁹

3. Finally, there is a sonority referred to as the *altered dominant chord*, which combines the V chords (with upper extensions) of C minor and C blues. As the name implies, it is usually used as a dominant chord (Ex. 13–17).

Example 13–17.

    a. Stacked in thirds.   **b.** In stepwise order.

A♭ or A♮ can be used; both are found in the "altered scale."

The arranger then, can control the number of upper extensions, the nature of those extensions, and the degree of blues influence in a given passage.

Chord Substitution

The concepts of upper extensions, frequent chord-tone alteration, and free use of inversion (stemming from the traditional improvised string bass line) led jazz writers and performers quite naturally to *chord substitution*. This involves the replacement of a chord in the source tune with a different chord or two or more chords. Chord substitution is valuable to the jazz arranger in that much source material is from the pop or show literature and has very simple chord qualities and relations. These qualities and relations usually must be made more sophisticated if they are to project a contemporary jazz style.

The following are various SATB *a cappella* settings of the spiritual *Swing Low, Sweet Chariot*, illustrating the more common chord substitutions.[2] Of course, substitutions must not conflict harmonically with the melody, although the melody may be adjusted slightly to accommodate the substitution.

Example 13–18a. The source arranged for SATB *a cappella*.

1. Add diatonic sevenths to most chords.

Example 13–18b.

---

[2]Another illustration of the reharmonization of a given melody, used primarily to show choral directors various types of contemporary choral textures, can be found in Carl Strommen's *The Contemporary Chorus, A Director's Guide for the Jazz-Rock Choir* (Sherman Oaks, CA: Alfred Publishing Company, 1980).

2. Substitute other diatonic chords which have two notes in the triad in common with those of the source chord (Ex. 13–18c). This is particularly useful in avoiding an overabundance of I chords.

Substitute iii   for   I
          vi   for   I
          V   for   vii
         (vii   for   V)
          ii   for   IV
         (IV   for   ii)

Example 13–18c.

3. Just prior to a given chord, insert *its* V^7 (this does not work prior to vii, since it is too unstable to provide a satisfactory chord of resolution). Example 13–18d shows this application to Example 13–18b; the technique could also be applied to the chords generated in Example 13–18c.

Example 13–18d.

4. Every major-minor seventh (Mm7) chord (e.g., g-b-d-f) may be considered a temporary V^7, and may be replaced by ii^7–V^7 (e.g., G^7 replaced by $D\text{-}^7 \, G^7$). This increases the harmonic rhythm, as two chords take the place of one. (Example 13–18e is based on Example 13–18d above.)

Example 13–18e.

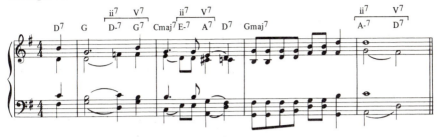

5. A Mm^7 chord may be replaced by a Mm^7 chord whose root is a tritone away. Note that each of the tritone substitutions in Example 13–18f (based on Example 13–18d above) employs a ♭5 (C$\sharp^{7(♭5)}$ and A♭$^{7(♭5)}$). The ♭5 is not essential to this substitution principle but does make the harmonic relations smoother by virtue of a common tone. (For example, the 5th of a C$^{\sharp7}$ chord is $g^\sharp$, whereas the 5th of C$^{\sharp7(♭5)}$ is g, which is also in the preceding G chord and the following C chord.) However, in this example the ♭5's are necessary, as in each case they are the melody notes.

Example 13–18f.

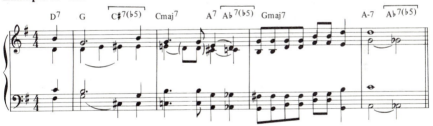

6. Chords may be generated from the interaction of the melody and a chromatic bass line (Ex. 13–18g). Note that in the illustration the bass line is designed so that at the melodic cadence, the bass note forms the root (*A*) of a structurally important ii^7 chord. The clearly directed bass line compensates for the unusual harmonic progression.

Example 13–18g.

7. The source harmonic progression may again be discarded, and a root motion by fifths substituted. The chord should be in root position to provide clear down-by-fifths motion while sometimes reinterpreting the melodic pitches as upper extensions.

Example 13–18h.

8. Several of the above techniques may be combined so that the bass moves chromatically while forming the root of each chord. The predictability of this motion is broken, and forward motion is aided, by interspersing and resolving V^7 chords. Because of the intense chromaticism created by this technique, it should be used sparingly. Care must be taken to avoid many parallel 7ths and 9ths, as they are especially difficult to sing (Ex. 13–18i).

As demonstrated by the inner voices of bars 2 and 3 of this illustration, any of these settings can be intensified even further by the interpolation of diatonic and chromatic nonharmonic tones.

Example 13–18i.

9. The entire harmonic progression may be replaced by *quartal parallelism*—chords constructed of perfect fourth intervals from the melody downward. Unity is achieved by the consistency of intervals and texture, rather than by conventional root motion. Quartal parallelism should be used sparingly due to its homogeneity, and only when the conventional harmonic direction is to be suspended (Ex. 13–18j).

This technique is not as effective when there is much repetition of a melodic pitch, since the entire chord also repeats. However, in the example, note that while the "d" melody note is held in the last bar, the accompanying voices move on in another mode for interest while maintaining the perfect fourth relation among themselves.

Example 13–18j.

Although the blues began with a simple harmonic structure which can be maintained in an arrangement, the twelve-bar blues form has been subjected to substitutions using the above techniques alone or in combination. For example, Charlie Parker's *Blues for Alice* exhibits a combination of the first five techniques described above (Ex. 13–19).

Example 13–19. Chord changes for Charlie Parker's *Blues for Alice*

SIMPLE BLUES CHANGES:	F^7	./.	./.	./.	
PARKER'S CHANGES:	FMa^7	$E^{-7(\flat5)} A^{7(\flat9)}$	$D^{-7} G^7$	$C^{-7} F^7$	
	$B\flat^7$	./.	F^7	./.	
	$B\flat^7$	$B^{\flat-7} E^{\flat7}$	$A^{-7} D^7$	$A\flat^7 D\flat^7$	
	C^7	./.	F^7	C^7	
	G^{-7}	C^7	$FMa^7 D^{-7}$	$G^{-7} C^7$	

Lastly, the blues style can be injected into a non-blues arrangement (for that more earthy intensity) by substituting Mm^7 and $Mm^{7(\#9)}$ chords for major chords where appropriate. Again, we turn in Example 13–20 to *Swing Low, Sweet Chariot*, which, because it is a spiritual, adapts well emotionally to the blues idiom.

Example 13–20.

Above all, in using chord substitutions, the arranger must remain sensitive to the style of the source, the scope of the arrangement, and the underlying harmonic direction of the passage in which substitutions are to be made.

Voicings

The voicing of the choral parts is an important aspect of arranging in all idioms, but certain considerations will be addressed here which are unique to jazz styles.

1. Register   While the conventional vocal ranges apply to jazz singers, most jazz choral styles strive for a warm, cohesive sound. The tessitura of women's parts should stay in the low to middle register—below the women's break (around c^2) except in loud passages. To contribute to the cohesiveness and to maintain a buoyant quality in swing arrangements, men's parts should be written in the middle to high register, with care taken not to overwrite the tenors in their bright register (above d^1).

2. Dividing parts   As mentioned earlier, there may be a great temptation to divide one or more of the choir parts in order to include upper extensions in a voicing. For the average choir, divide a part only for a brief passage and only when the thicker texture warrants it and smooth voice leading makes it possible. Only divide the soprano or bass part, as those sections are the largest in most choirs and will allow division without the parts getting too thin.

Generally, the arranger should maintain the four-voice (or less) texture in an SATB arrangement. The inclusion of an upper extension will contribute to the overtone structure of the voicing, making it quite dense without dividing any parts. In certain circumstances, the root may be omitted from the voicing—particularly if it is present in the accompaniment—thus freeing a part for an upper extension. Voicing decisions should depend more upon which pitches of a given chord should sound and in what register, rather than how many pitches.

3. Arrangement of pitches   Harmonic clarity is best achieved when the pitches of the voicing are ordered so as to reinforce, as overtones, the chord root. The voicing with the clearest harmonic intent, then, would be voiced from the bass up: root, perfect 5th, major 3rd (above the root), minor 7th, major 9th, etc. Harmonic clarity is most desirable at cadences, at points of modulation, and when the harmonic progression is unconventional.

However, voice leading and a desire to vary harmonic clarity from one sonority to the next will usually dictate reordering of the chord tones in a voicing. For example, the progression ii-V-I can be realized in several ways, three of which are illustrated in Example 13–21.

Example 13–21a is the clearest in its harmonic progression, consisting only of root position 7th chords (plus the 9th in the V chord). Example 13–21b is less stable and less clear in harmonic intent in that the three chords are in inversion and the second chord has no root; the 9th that is added to the final I chord creates additional tension in that it forms the interval of a second with the root.

Example 13–21. Three realizations of the ii–V–I progression.

a.

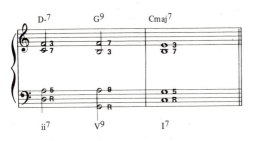

b.

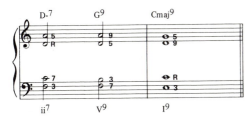

c.

Example 13–21c is the least clear in its harmonic intent in that the 11th replaces a more stable chord tone in each chord, the root is omitted from the V chord, and the configuration of the ii chord suggests quartal (built in 4ths) harmony while the upper three notes of both the V and I suggest triads unrelated to the chord roots.

It was mentioned earlier that the root may be omitted from the choral voicing of a chord (unless, of course, the melody note is the root). This is particularly common in "up swing" arrangements, where it provides buoyancy and forward motion, as demonstrated in Example 13–22. The root is usually in the accompaniment.

Example 13–22.

Amidst such manipulation two concerns arise. First, for melodic clarity the interval of at least a 3rd should separate the melody line from other voices. Second, just as such rearrangement of chord tones creates ambiguity for the listener, the ambiguity makes hearing and reproducing the lines difficult for the performer. Smooth voice leading and frequent interjection of harmonic clarity will provide the singer with needed security. The amount of voicing manipulation is dependent above all on the experience of the choir.

FORMAL STRUCTURE

As in other idioms, a jazz arrangement is dependent upon its source for its essential formal design. Because of its roots and tradition, two designs predominate in the literature: The AABA form and the blues form.

AABA Form

The great majority of vocal jazz arrangements are settings of single-verse show tunes, most of which exhibit the AABA form, with each letter representing eight bars. Traditionally, an arrangement in which a singer was accompanied by a big band, small group, or solo piano, adhered to the format exhibited in Example 13–23.

Example 13–23.

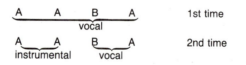

Because improvisation is essential to jazz, the instrumental section may have been an improvised solo, based on the chord changes of that section.

It is quite natural to employ this format in a jazz choir arrangement. The only difference is that the AA sections of the second time (the instrumental section above) may feature any of the following:

1. An instrumental soloist The part may be written out, but an improvised solo is more in keeping with the jazz tradition. (Nonetheless, most publishers require that the arranger write out a "suggested" solo, to provide a guide for the inexperienced improvisor.) Chord symbols should be included whether or not the suggested solo is written out. Frequently the choir will provide a background texture for the soloist, often for the second of the eight bars. This allows a smooth transition to the vocalists predominating in the B section to follow (Ex. 13–24).

2. A written-out section for several instrumentalists, alone or interacting with the choir See Example 13–25.

3. A vocal soloist The same holds here as for the instrumental soloist discussed under 1 above. The vocal solo may use phrases from the song, improvised lyrics, or scat syllables. It should be clear from the construction of the lyrics and melody that this section is not part of the original tune.

Example 13–24. Traditional (arr. K. Shaw): *Lonesome Road*

Example 13–25. Spence, Keith, and Bergman (arr. D. Riley and D. Wilson): *Nice 'n' Easy*

4. A written-out section for several vocalists   The melody may be dramatically altered from the original, or the choir can sing scat syllables as in Example 13–26.

After the choir reenters in the B section, there is sometimes a modulation into the last A section for a dramatic shift. The final A section may be revoiced and louder to provide the arrangement with a sense of climax or arrival.

Example 13–26. Cahn, Stordahl, and Weston (arr. K. Shaw): *Day by Day*

If the song has more than one verse, the above treatment of the second time through is inappropriate. So that the second verse may be projected clearly, the melody should remain intact for the AA of the second verse, but a texture change (men or women alone, or solo voice, or solo voice with inconspicuous vocal background) would probably be necessary for variety.

Blues Form

Many vocal and instrumental tunes are based on the twelve-bar blues form. The basic harmonic structure of each "chorus" of the blues was shown in Example 13–19. Melodically, each chorus is usually comprised of three four-bar phrases, with the second a repetition of the first, and the third different. Each chorus is a new verse but essentially the same melody, and thus textural variation is required every few verses. After two or three verses, it is common to feature an improvised[3] solo lasting one or more choruses. The various instrumentalists can each take a short solo, or a vocalist (particularly in a fast blues) can sing a scat solo. For added excitement, just before the singers reenter with the last verses, the drummer might "trade fours" with the soloist. This means that the instrumental or vocal soloist would improvise for four bars, then *all* would stop while the drummer would improvise for four bars, then the soloist, then the drummer, and so forth. The form of the source would remain intact, and the drummer would be the last one to improvise before all return to the "head" or main melody.

Endings

Codas may be as individual as the arrangements they serve to close. However, there is a brief ending, know as a *tag*, that is so stock, or common, in its use that it has almost become a stylistic trait. It involves tunes where the final four bars are devoted to the progression: $ii^7/V^7/I/I$. The stock tag involves converting the final measure into a V^7 of ii and then repeating the last four bars. This can repeat as long as the energy and excitement continue to build (Ex. 13–27). To ensure such build, the arranger should write out the repeats including a new element each time.

Example 13–27.

IN THE KEY OF G:	A-⁷(ii⁷)	D⁷(V⁷)	GMa⁷(I)	E⁷(V⁷/ii)
REPEATS	{ A-⁷ { A-⁷	D⁷ D⁷	GMa⁷ GMa⁷	E⁷ E⁷
VERY LAST TIME	{ A-⁷	D⁷	GMa⁷	GMa⁷

---

[3] Any "improvised" solo section can be written out, as mentioned earlier.

MODEL ARRANGEMENT

Nice 'n' Easy (Spence, Keith, and
Bergman; arr. D. Riley and
D. Wilson) (Music contained in
Appendix II)

The basic form of the song *Nice 'n' Easy* is $AA^1 BA^2$, with all sections eight measures long except the A^2, which is twelve measures long. The overall structure for the arrangement of this song is as follows:

ARRANGEMENT FORM	Intro	A	A¹	B	A²	A	A¹	B	A²
TOTAL MEASURES	4	8	8	8	12	8	8	8	12 + 4 (extension)
MEASURE NUMBERS ON SCORE		5	13	21	29	41	49	57	65

Many of the techniques discussed in this chapter exist in this arrangement:

Tempo and "swing feel" markings
Intro: Interaction between instruments and voices
    m. 5–12:   Two-beat feel in accompaniment; voices in unison
    m. 13–20:   Increased syncopation in voices; vocal texture thickens
    m. 21–28:   Syncopation accented; four-voice texture which then thins for return of A section
    m. 29–40:   Articulation markings:
            ascending smear (m. 33)
            fall off (m. 37)
            ghost (m. 38)
    m. 41–56:   (A and A¹ sections of second chorus): Phrases exchanged between instruments and voices (first suggested in intro); chord substitution for reharmonization and increased harmonic rhythm; the use of scat syllables
    m. 57–64:   Straight ahead, four-beat feel in the accompaniment
    m. 65–end: Return to two-beat feel; active syncopation and varied articulation in the tag (last four measures)

As the conception of this arrangement follows the "nice and easy" nature of the song, the chord extensions and alterations are purposely limited. The accompaniment of this arrangement will be discussed in Chapter 15.

ARRANGING EXERCISES

Address the following with regard to at least the first eight bars of the song *I Could Write a Book*, found in Appendix I.

1. Through syncopation and other rhythmic alterations, transform the rhythm of the melody so that it suggests a relaxed swing style.

2. Transform the rhythm of the melody so that it suggests a smooth bossa nova style.

3. To the melody (or to your version as transformed in exercise 1), add at least four jazz pitch or articulation markings which would aid the performer in capturing the swing style.

4. Place the melody in the soprano part; voice altos, tenors, and basses. Do not double long-held melody pitches, and be sure that at least the 3rd and 7th of each chord are sounding. Do not write an accompaniment, but assume one would be present.

5. Rewrite the excerpt, substituting for some Mm7 chords a Mm7 chord whose root is a tritone away. Adjust chord symbols to reflect desired chord alterations ($^{b}5$, #9, etc.) as needed.

6. Set the melody as an *a cappella* ballad in the SATB texture, using chord upper extensions where voice leading permits. Indicate chord symbols (including any extensions or alterations) in parentheses above the excerpt.

CHAPTER FOURTEEN

COUNTRY, ROCK,
AND POP
VOCAL STYLES

DUE TO THEIR IMMEDIATE FOLK ROOTS, country, rock, and pop styles tend to be simpler than jazz in at least certain respects. These styles will be considered individually in this chapter, keeping in mind that mass communication has served to blur the distinctions among styles.

Country Music

With its roots in the folk music of the British Isles via the hills of the southeastern United States, country music (and country and western music, which is also rooted in the cowboy songs of the West) relies harmonically upon triads of the I, IV, and V chords, plus an occasional secondary dominant chord (usually V^7/V) for color. It is this unabashed simplicity that evokes its folk roots while providing an uncluttered musical vehicle for the text, often the most important aspect of a song.

Vocal textures should be correspondingly simple, relying on unisons, triads, homophony, and brief counter-material. Characteristic of this style is the frequent use of the perfect fourth as a harmonic interval (chord root with fifth below), as seen in Example 14–1, at the words "tall and six."

The major mode predominates in this style. Minor mode melodies are often Dorian or Aeolian, to include the flatted seventh scale degree. Melodic inflections are common in country music but, unlike the chromatic blues inflections, are essentially diatonic, due to their European source:

I'm   go - in'   home.

Example 14–1. Connor (arr. D. Riley and D. Wilson): *Grandma's Feather Bed*

© 1980 Cherry River Music Co. Reprinted by permission of
Cherry Lane Music Co.

This whole-step sliding, which can be heard in most country-influenced music, is fun for singers to execute at a fast tempo. At a slower tempo, where it may be rhythmically awkward for a chorus, the figure may be written out:

The rhythm of most country music adheres to an even eighth-note pulse (and therefore, unlike swing music, should be sung exactly as written), although a two-beat swing or triplet feel can be found in certain moderate or slow tunes. Fast tunes which capture the energy of traditional banjo or fiddle music rely on sixteenth notes and occasional syncopation where they enhance text declamation (Ex. 14–2).

The story line of a country song is often projected in strophic form or verse-refrain alternation. In an arrangement, interest can be achieved by different choral combinations (including solos) for each verse, followed by a homophonic refrain. In a long arrangement, at least one modulation should be considered, as well as simple, yet energetic, devices such as ostinatos. Something fresh can happen in the final refrain (repetition, rhythmic or dynamic change, descant, etc.) to generate an exciting ending.

Rock Music

It is impossible to categorize all types of rock music. Essentially, the various types are some combination of *rhythm and blues* (an urbanized extension of the blues) and *gospel music* ("Africanized" Protestant hymn music) on the one hand, and country music and show music on the other. Since the 1950s, rock has been

Example 14–2. Connor (arr. D. Riley and D. Wilson): *Grandma's Feather Bed*

© 1980 Cherry River Music Co. Reprinted by permission of Cherry Lane Music Co.

the most popular American dance music, relying heavily on a steady, even eighth-note pulse in $\frac{4}{4}$ meter, with emphasis on the second and fourth beats.

From rhythm and blues, certain rock styles borrowed the basic blues scale, inflections, and progression (see Chapter 13), causing the seventh, when present in the I and IV chords, to be "flatted." Certain early rock was based upon I–vi–ii–V and other progressions from show music, or the I–IV–V progressions of country music. Much later, rock came to rely upon "vamp"-style ostinatos, often based upon modes such as the mixolydian (major scale with a flatted seventh degree). As seen in example 14-3, the mixolydian mode causes the I chord (C) *and* the ♭VII chord (B♭) to be major triads. (The e♭ in the second measure is a blues inflection.)

The dorian mode is often used when the minor quality (with raised sixth degree) is desired:

While an airy, rootless choral sound is often desirable in jazz to contribute to the subtle swing or bossa feel, rock is more direct and "earthy." This is achieved in choral writing through much unison or octave doubling, "strong" intervals such as fifths and fourths (sometimes in parallel motion), and root position chords. Most chords are restricted to simple triads or the seventh chords described above, although ninths are sometimes inserted into the accompaniment.

The pitch material in a rock song is often repetitive, or encompasses a narrow range. This may serve the text well and can even create a desired hypnotic effect, but may not transcribe well for chorus. (Source material in this style should still be selected according to its melodic integrity so that it will "sing" well.) Melodic inflections, like other aspects of style, depend upon the roots of the source material.

Example 14–3. Anka and Harris (arr. K. Shaw): *Jubilation*

Rock coming from the black tradition may use more blues inflections, while rock from the white tradition often employs embellishments which are diatonic in the given mode:

a. With e^b blues inflection

b. With d diatonic embellishment

Rock melodies often gain a feeling of angularity through sharp articulations and the use of silence between words or even syllables. Two sonorities have emerged in rock music which should be part of an arranger's vocabulary:

The first sonority usually serves as a V(sus4) chord in the key of F. The second sonority, derived from the blues minor-major third ($d\sharp$ /e), can be constructed on a I or V chord, to give a very strident or plaintive quality.

Example 14–4 illustrates many aspects of the rock style discussed above. Note (a) the repetitive nature of the harmonic progression; (b) the simple melodic line which captures the emotion of the text; (c) the triadic voicings moving in parallel motion for strength; (d) the use of G mixolydian (major with flatted seventh) mode; (e) the use of b♭ in the melody to create a "blue note" against the b♮ in the accompaniment's G triad. These elements of pitch contribute to the strong "edge" that rock music can have, though certainly all rock music does not employ all of these elements.

Of primary importance in creating the exuberance or pain of rock music is rhythm, specifically, syncopation and the layering of a rhythmic figure in one part upon a different figure in another part. In fact, it may be in part to counterbalance the rhythmic complexity of most rock styles that melodic and harmonic materials are usually simple. In Example 14–5, the melodic elements are rather static, while the rhythmic complexity within and among parts (including the accompaniment) provides great vitality.

Example 14–4. Anka and Harris (arr. K. Shaw): *Jubilation*

Example 14–5. Johnston (arr. A. Billingsley): *Long Train Running*

The *rock ballad* is similar in design, but is played at a slow tempo. While the pulse is maintained exactly, the syncopation loses its impact at the slower tempo, and interest is derived from more lyrical melodies and complex choral voicings, including major sevenths and ninths (Ex. 14–6). Note in the example the crucial role of the piano in maintaining a steady pulse while contributing to the overall lyricism.

The formal design of rock songs varies considerably, depending, again, on their roots. Many follow the form of the twelve-bar blues, some are verse and refrain, and some follow the AABA form of many standard show tunes.

A common way for a rock song to end on a recording is to fade out while a short passage is played over and over. This fade-out technique rarely succeeds in an arrangement that is to be performed live. Therefore, a suitable stronger ending should replace it, possibly repeating the same last line as on the recording but

Example 14–6. Linzer and Wolfert (arr. D. Riley and D. Wilson): *I Believe in You and Me*

bringing it to a final cadence. (Publishers often like the final words to include the song's title.) The last few bars can slow down as long as the excitement is maintained by thicker sonorities, louder dynamics, and the like.

In adapting a rock tune to a choral setting, the arranger must be cognizant of all the components that provide a given song's energy and shape. Several recordings of rock music, for example, rely heavily upon intricate electric bass and drum patterns, layered colors and textures often produced by string orchestras or synthesizers, and vocal acrobatics performable only by an experienced soloist. An arrangement should capture the essence of the recording (particularly if it might be well known to the audience), while developing the strengths of choral writing in order to create different but equal energy. Intricate rhythms and embellishments generally should be simplified, while choral voicings and simple counter-material may be introduced. The electric bass and drum set should be included in the arrangement, if feasible, to help capture the style.

Pop Music

A style even more encompassing than rock, pop music finds its strongest roots in the sentimental ballad, popular in nineteenth-century America, which influenced the show tune of this century. Today it may also contain jazz or rock elements.

The melodies of pop music are usually lyrical and flowing (made even smoother by pop vocal stylists originally referred to as *crooners*). Harmonically, pop relies essentially upon triads and seventh chords (and ninths without sevenths) in a diatonic setting, often with one or two dramatic modulations to provide interest. It is rhyth-

Example 14–7. Shire and A. and M. Bergman (arr. J. Nowak): *The Promise*

mically simple with occasional syncopation, either in swing or even eighth-note style.

Pop music frequently relies upon the rhythm section (piano, guitar, bass, and drums) of jazz, rock, and country styles, but these instruments merely provide background support for the main melodic material without a sense of rhythmic propulsion. Example 14–7 illustrates typical pop text, the very accessible melody, and diatonic harmony. The voicings are basically seventh chords with some passing, suspensive, and anticipatory material. The rhythms smoothly follow the text declamation and comfortably support the meter and phrasing of two-bars-plus-two-bars. The piano accompaniment supports the vocal material while contributing to the sense of meter and to the flowing nature of the music.

Because of the commercial success of pop music, several publishers have created "pop chorals" catalogues. These arrangements tend to be light in nature, with gentle syncopation and simple harmonic and contrapuntal textures whether or not the source material is actually a popular song.

SUMMARY AND SYNTHESIS

The cross-pollination of musical styles has led to several hybrid forms. In idioms such as those discussed in this chapter which rely heavily on aural transmission and improvisation, this process happens quickly and frequently. A synthesis of the styles discussed in this chapter can create interesting new styles.

Example 14–8 demonstrates how one source melody might be set to capture the various styles. The characteristics of the first three should now be clear. The fourth may be considered country-rock because it is merely the country setting (Ex. 14–8a) with syncopation and articulation intensified to suggest the rock style. The fifth may be considered jazz-rock because it employs harmonically rich jazz voicings as well as rock-style syncopation.

A common and noble reason for arranging in these styles is that the source material may be well known to audiences and performers. The arranger must decide whether the material adapts well to the choral setting by simplifying certain parameters, while enhancing others. Next, stylistic concerns must be addressed so that appropriate and consistent voicings, embellishments, and rhythmic figures capture the essence of country, rock, pop, jazz, or a synthesis of two or more styles.

Example 14–8. One source melody set in various popular styles.

a. Moderate country.

b. Moderate rock.

c. Moderate (pop style).

d. Country-rock.

e. Jazz-rock (even 8ths).

ARRANGING EXERCISES

Arrange the first four measures of the source melody *Wade in the Water* (in Appendix I) in various styles as requested below. Do not write an accompaniment, but assume at least a piano part would accompany each of your settings. Use inflections as appropriate.

1. Country or country-rock style, in an SAB setting. Include country-type inflections.

2. Rock-style, in an SATB setting. Rests may be inserted mid-phrase for emphasis. Em-D vamp may replace given chord changes.

3. Rock-ballad style. Assume the necessary eighth-note pulse is provided by the piano accompaniment.

4. Pop style with a gentle, even eighth-note feel. The melody may be altered somewhat to add to its lyricism.

CHAPTER FIFTEEN

THE ACCOMPANIMENT IN JAZZ AND OTHER POPULAR STYLES

IN CHAPTER FOUR IT WAS STATED THAT A RHYTHMIC PATTERN in the accompaniment alone can establish an arrangement's style. This chapter will focus on the rhythmic patterns, pitch inflections, and voicings used in the accompaniment to establish the various so-called popular styles. We will begin with a discussion of the traditional accompanying ensemble, referred to, aptly, as the *rhythm section.*

THE INSTRUMENTS OF THE RHYTHM SECTION

A piano accompaniment alone can capture the styles discussed here, but the more complete the rhythm section, the more intricate the rhythmic layering can be and the greater the coloristic and dynamic range available to the arranger. As choral arrangements in these styles have become more popular, publishers have begun to include, with arrangements, parts for an entire rhythm section—piano/guitar, bass, and drums. (These parts are included in the score, but the bass player and drummer usually receive separate parts to avoid frequent page turns.)

Piano

As in other styles, the piano provides pitch support—harmonies, entering vocal pitches, and the like—when functioning in a rhythm section. It also contributes to the rhythmic style, sometimes having its own repetitive pattern as in a rock tune, or subtly suggesting syncopation as in a relaxed jazz tune.

Some musicians prefer the electric piano to the acoustic piano for reasons of color and volume (and portability). The keyboard synthesizer rarely replaces the piano, but can be added for unusual and colorful effects, including string sonorities.

Guitar

The guitar can be used to provide chordal rhythmic patterns or melodic lines. For reasons of style and balance, the electric guitar is used in the rhythm section, although a strummed or arpeggiated acoustic guitar may be appropriate for quiet, folk-country style arrangements.

The guitar part is written in treble clef, sounding one octave below. Its six strings are tuned as follows:

Most arrangements have a written-out piano part, with chord symbols for the guitarist, assuming the latter will improvise appropriate voicings, melodic fills, and solos. While our discussion will focus on the role of the piano, most of the considerations would also apply to the guitar, should the arranger wish to write specific figures for that instrument.

Bass

The string bass replaced the tuba in early jazz and is still the appropriate bass instrument for music evolving from jazz styles of the 1930s, 1940s, and 1950s. It provides a strong attack to the pitch (thereby contributing to the "groove"), though its size limits its activity. It is an acoustic instrument, but may be amplified.

The electric bass is preferable for rock music and certain Latin (here meaning Central *and* South American) music where speed or sustained tone is desirable. Because of its size and similarity to the guitar, it is more likely to be found in "young" ensembles than the string bass.

The part for both types of bass (the arranger needn't distinguish) is written in bass clef, sounding one octave below. Its four strings are tuned as follows:

Most bass players read chord symbols, though it is recommended that at least a few bars of a suggested part be written out since the bass provides the "bottom" for the ensemble, and thus its pitches affect how all the choral and instrumental voicings are heard above.

Drums

The term *drums* is used to label the drum set or *kit*—a collection of percussion instruments, including cymbals as well as drums. An aerial view of the typical setup is:

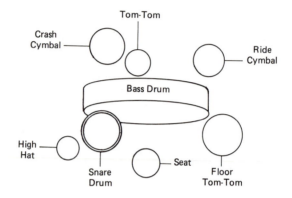

The drummer uses sticks, or brushes for softer pieces.

Added percussion instruments, such as maracas, claves, shaker, and tambourine, can also be played by the drummer (if not occupied by the set) or by other members of the ensemble. These instruments are typically used in Latin-oriented music, including bossa novas.

Most drummers read a rhythm staff, which usually includes only the most fundamental figures (the notation is not yet standardized):

It is important to keep the drum part simple, primarily indicating figures basic to the arrangement's style; an accomplished drummer will embellish appropriately. It is also usually only necessary to write out two bars of the desired patterns. If later in the arrangement a specific effect is desired, it can be inserted. If, for example, the vocal rhythms are to be reinforced at a given point, it is necessary only to write:

The notation at "a" indicates that the basic style is to be continued; at "b," the drummer is to emphasize the written rhythm.

Example 15–1.

INSTRUMENTAL ROLES

The role of the rhythm section is to emphasize the style characteristics discussed in Chapters 13 and 14. Here, we will examine the contributions made by each instrument of the rhythm section in the various styles.

Jazz: Swing

There are two basic swing styles: two-beat and "straight ahead." The two-beat style has its roots in the solo, stride piano style of the early part of the twentieth century. At its simplest, the accompaniment might look like that shown in Example 15–1. The characteristic bass line has root and fifth on the first and third beats, respectively, while the right-hand chord emphasizes beats 2 and 4.

If a bass is added, it will play the roots and fifths, possibly in a more intensified rhythm (♩. ♪ ♩. ♪). The drums can play variations on the following:

"Straight-ahead swing, four to the bar" refers to the fact that the bass plays four quarter notes each bar, thereby intensifying the root motion. In Example 15–2 the bass pitches are primarily chord tones, with roots on the beat where the chords change. The piano may emphasize beats 2 and 4, but there is much more syncopation and space between chords than in the two-beat style. Because the bass plays many roots, the piano voicings are essentially rootless, to maintain the "up in the air" quality of swing music, and often contain upper extensions—ninths and thirteenths, sometimes with chromatic alteration.

As in two-beat style, the drums' high hat emphasizes beats 2 and 4, but quarter-note and swing eighth-note "time" is kept on the ride cymbal. Greater intensity is achieved by freeing the bass drum to punctuate rhythmic figures in counterpoint with the snare drum.

Example 15–2. Spence, Keith, and Bergman (arr. D. Riley and D. Wilson) *Nice 'n' Easy*

If only piano is available, it must accomplish all of the above tasks. Note in Example 15–3 how the left hand "walks," while the right hand supplies the rootless harmony, syncopation, and a certain melodic shape. Pay particular attention to the smooth voice leading in the right-hand part.

Example 15–3. Mancini and Bricusse (arr. S. Fredrickson): *I Like the Look*

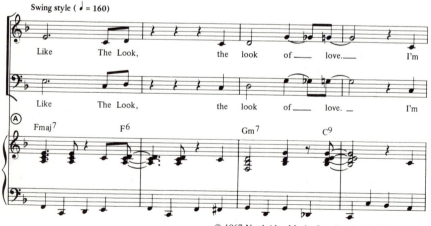

Example 15–4.

Two styles related to swing are *shuffle* and *gospel*. Shuffle is similar to straight-ahead swing, but the piano right hand tends to play every offbeat (Ex. 15–4).

Gospel is closer to two-beat swing (although sometimes in $\frac{3}{4}$) but maintains a definite triplet feel (Ex. 15–5).

Example 15–5. Gospel accompaniment.

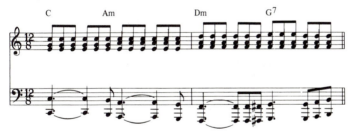

Whatever the swing style, if the music is blues-oriented, blues inflections can be found in the accompaniment, as well as in the vocal parts:

Jazz: Bossa Nova

The instrumental roles for bossa nova are very similar to those in two-beat, but with an even eighth-note feel and frequent, but relaxed, syncopations in the piano part (Ex. 15–6).

Example 15–6. Strommen: *New Bossa*

Note that in the above example a drum part has been suggested. It is likely that in performance a bass would be included as well, playing essentially the bass-clef portion of the piano part. If there is a bass, this bass-clef portion should not also be played by the pianist (in most *jazz* styles) so that the music does not become too bottom-heavy. Looked at from another standpoint, published arrangements often have bass parts written out which are doubled in the piano part. Many arrangers and performers do not realize that the part is not to be doubled in jazz-style music, but is included in the piano part only in case no bass is available.

Example 15–7.

Rock Music

There are too many styles of rock to categorize here. In terms of the rhythm section, rock differs from swing in general in that:

1. All articulations are sharper, sometimes made even more dramatic by short rests within a phrase.

2. Rhythmic figures are more repetitive—often one figure per bar repeated over several bars.

3. Many chord roots are desirable in both the piano and the bass to create a solid, ''earthy'' sound; triads and major-minor seventh chords predominate.

4. The bass line can be very active in terms of both rhythm and pitch.

5. Whereas, for the drummer, the focus in playing jazz is largely in the cymbals, in rock, it is more in the drums. The bass drum may play an important rhythmic pattern, and the snare drum replaces the high hat for the stylistic stress on beats 2 and 4; the cymbals keep an eighth-note pulse, either on the closed high hat or louder on the ride cymbal, with occasional accents on the crash cymbal.

Three examples of rock-style accompaniments are given below, each in a different tempo.

Example 15–8.

a. Fast rock—Anka and Harris (arr. K. Shaw): *Jubilation*

(Continued next page)

Note in the above example the repetitive nature of all accompanying figures. Chord roots predominate, reinforced by simple triads within a modal context. The bass drum is loud and persistent, matched by the snare drum on beats 2 and 4, and colored by even eighth notes on the closed high hat.

b. Medium rock (funk)—Leinbach (arr. M. Huff): *Keep on Rollin'*

Here, again, the patterns are repetitive, and the seventh chord is in root position throughout. In this slower tempo the bass assumes a more active and syncopated role, while the drums are enhanced by the striking of the high hat, first closed (+), then open (o). Note the indication "guitar in," suggesting it will play *ad lib* or in a rhythm similar to that of the piano.

c. Rock ballad—Linzer and Wolfert (arr. D. Riley and D. Wilson): *I Believe in You and Me*

The accompaniment for a rock ballad requires an even pulse clearly defined, root position chords, sometimes colored by added ninths or suspended fourths, and occasional syncopation.

Country Music

Traditional music of the hill country of the southeastern United States is usually accompanied by banjo, guitar, fiddle, and tub bass. Choral arrangements suggesting this style should use piano (and bass) in a triadic, chordal, and rhythmic accompaniment, as shown in Example 15–9.

Example 15–9. Connor (arr. D. Riley and D. Wilson): *Grandma's Feather Bed*

This *bluegrass* music merged with cowboy and other folk styles, and then with more broadly based styles, before it became widely popular. *Country music* has come to refer to songs in the two-beat swing style, the slow gospel $\frac{12}{8}$ style, or the rock style, whose texts convey a "down-home" story and whose melodic line adopts certain country inflections. The writing for the rhythm section, then, would reflect the appropriate style, possibly with strong reliance on the electric guitar. As in the vocal writing, the accompaniment can incorporate country inflections:

Pop Music

In accompanying pop songs, a rhythm section should adopt one of the basic styles discussed above. The vocal line must always predominate in a lyrical fashion, though the piano may double the melody occasionally.

ARRANGING EXERCISES

1. Write a solo piano accompaniment to the following choral excerpt in a two-beat style.

Autumn Leaves, words by Johnny Mercer and music by Joseph Kosma. © 1947 Ardmore Music. Reprinted with permission of Morley Music Co.

2. Write complete parts for a rhythm section (piano, bass, and drum; optional guitar rhythms over chord changes above piano part) to accompany the following choral excerpt in four-beat (walking bass) style. The piano part can be independent of the choral writing; the bass should "walk"; therefore, the low register of the piano should not be used. The drum part need only suggest the style, with at least two measures of cymbal (high hat and ride) figures. Refer to Examples 15–2 or 15–8b for score setup.

As Time Goes By, words and music by Herman Hupfeld. © 1931 (renewed) Warner Bros. Inc. All rights reserved. Used by permission.

3. Write a solo piano accompaniment to the following rock setting. Make the figures repetitive and, if desired, the bass line active. Include blues inflections where appropriate.

4. Write a solo piano accompaniment to the following setting of a pop ballad. Maintain the eighth-note motion, doubling the melody where appropriate.

CHAPTER SIXTEEN

ARRANGING WITH SMALL INSTRUMENTAL ENSEMBLES

ONCE THE ARRANGER HAS BECOME ADEPT AT WRITING keyboard accompaniments, adding other instruments may be considered. This chapter will discuss how these instruments can serve to focus upon the thematic material of a given song, enhance the mood, and reinforce the style of the arrangement.

The role of these instruments in choral arrangements is an extension of the keyboard accompaniment's usual role: to provide introductions, interludes, and endings; to fill the space at vocal phrase endings and lead into the next vocal phrase; to unify the arrangement through return of instrumental figures, sections, and textures. Whatever their functions, once instruments are introduced, they must play an integral part in the arrangement. Care must also be taken to write parts which are *idiomatic* (comfortably played on the designated instrument) and in keeping with the style of the arrangement. For in-depth study of these facets of instrumental writing, the reader is referred to an orchestration text or book on jazz-rock instrumental arranging. This chapter will discuss the addition of one instrument, two instruments, and then an ensemble, to a keyboard accompaniment.

ADDING ONE INSTRUMENT

The simplest way to add an instrument is to have it double a portion of the keyboard accompaniment, thereby making the added part optional and lending flexibility to the arrangement. In Example 16–1, a flute may double the top line of the piano

Example 16–1. Mallett (arr. D. Riley and D. Wilson): *Garden Song*

accompaniment in the introduction, interludes, and ending, thereby enhancing the pastoral quality of this metaphorical song about making a garden grow. Note that because the flute is a non-transposing instrument, its optional part can be indicated simply by directing the stems upward from the piano part.

When an instrument assumes a more independent role, it should be given a separate staff above the choral staves, transposed, if necessary, to the instrument's key. The flute line in Example 16–2, more independent than the one described above, provides an introduction which is then repeated exactly as a counter-line to the choral melody. The flute line was most likely conceived first as a counterline (to be sure that it would interact effectively with the chorus) and then placed as an introduction, with a different harmonic structure for variety.

Its independence established, the instrument in the example will be a dominant musical factor throughout the arrangement, providing figuration, interludes, and an ending, and allowing the keyboard part to concentrate on harmonic and rhythmic support.

ADDING TWO INSTRUMENTS

Two like instruments can share the same staff, with their notes sharing the same stem unless different rhythms demand the distinction of stems up for the first instrument and stems down for the second. Two staves should be used if the parts cross frequently, or, of course, if two different types of instruments are used.

In the piece, *Come before the Lord with Praise!* two trumpets join the keyboard to capture the mood and style of heraldry. This is accomplished in the introduction and first interlude through homophonic writing, with a predominance of open fifths in the trumpet parts and harmonic and rhythmic reinforcement in the keyboard part (Ex. 16–3a).

In the second interlude, the brass writing is imitative at first, using a melodic motive heard earlier in the choral parts, providing unity. It is purposefully repetitive in order to effect a smooth modulation (Ex. 16–3b, measures 1–4). This melodic pattern then becomes the material for still another texture: trumpets in canon with sopranos and altos (singing the first verse) against a countermelody in the men's part (singing the second verse) (Ex. 16–3b, last four measures).

Example 16–2. Crossman and Ireland (arr. D. Schack): *My Song Is Love Unknown*

Again, this last passage was most likely written before verses 1 and 2 were completed. The canon is effective, in part, because of the I–V harmonic progression in each measure of the example. The men's counter-line is constructed mostly of chord tones consonant with the women's part, and its stepwise nature provides good balance for, and contrast with, the triadic shape of the canonic material. While

Example 16–3a. Sleeth: *Come before the Lord with Praise!*

each line is simple, the overall texture is intricate and offers the first opportunity for the trumpets to sound with the chorus (and on the words "blow the trumpet"!)—thus providing the arrangement with a fresh combination and a sense of growth.

As in the example above, the text—even the title itself—will often suggest an instrument whose inclusion in the arrangement would enhance the performance. The arrangement of *When the Saints Go Marching In*, cited in Example 16–4, includes a second verse which begins "Oh, when the trumpets will sound the call" and a third verse which begins "The bells will ring, ring, ring." The respective verses are accompanied by a trumpet and orchestral bells, thus helping the listener to focus on the text, creating new color, filling the space between phrases, and enhancing the celebratory mood of the song. To provide an effective ending, both instruments join the chorus and piano, as shown in the example. Note that the writing for instruments of contrasting nature must be appropriate to each (here, long notes in the bells' part and a triadic "call" in the trumpet part) and must interact effectively with each other, as well as with the chorus (here, doubling the chorus and playing chord tones). Also, for practical as well as musical reasons, the level of instrumental writing should usually approximate that for the chorus: for example, the instrumental part in an arrangement for middle school chorus should be written for a player at the middle school level.

ADDING AN INSTRUMENTAL ENSEMBLE

The more instruments involved, the more they should be considered as an autonomous unit, providing the arrangement with substantial weight, breadth, and energy. Two representative and common styles, sacred and jazz-rock, have been chosen to illustrate characteristic approaches to incorporating the small ensemble in the arrangement.

Example 16–3b. Sleeth: *Come before the Lord with Praise!*

Example 16–4. Traditional (arr. R. Artman): *When the Saints Go Marching In*

Sacred Style

In sacred styles, an ensemble of four instruments of the same family is frequently chosen to interact with the church choir. The brass quartet (two trumpets and two trombones) is the usual ensemble for this role, based on the jubilant mood easily portrayed by brass instruments, as well as the likelihood of finding adequate players in the church community. Another possible ensemble is the string quartet, although proficient players may not be as readily available. The typical score setup is to place the voices on the top staves, the instrumental ensemble in the middle, and the organ on the bottom.

Perhaps the most frequent form used for brass or string quartet and choir is the *chorale concertato*. Essentially a multi-versed treatment of a familiar hymn tune, this form joins the forces of the choir, the instrumental quartet, the organ, and sometimes even the congregation. Typically, the first verse will be a unison treatment; middle verses can include all-women, all-men, or *a cappella* settings; the last verse will be unison with descant, possibly including the congregation, in a grand climax combining all forces. Aside from the obvious role in introductions and interludes, the ensemble may provide simple chordal support for the voices with or without the organ, the higher instruments may provide a countermelody for a particular verse, or the entire ensemble may provide complex animated homophonic or contrapuntal accompaniment to a unison verse (often the last).

The arrangement of the hymn *O God, Our Help in Ages Past* in Example 16–5 is scored for brass quartet (two trumpets and two trombones), timpani, organ, and SATB choir. After an introduction by organ and brass, the first three verses present increasingly complicated homophonic settings of the hymn tune, moving from unison to animated homophony. The fourth verse adds a trumpet counter-melody, while the fifth places the melody in the tenors. The example begins where an interlude restates the musical material from the introduction, leading into the unison sixth and last verse, which should be sung by both the choir and the congregation. The brass writing in the interlude moves from quasi-imitation and complex contrapuntal writing to a straightforward homophonic statement of the first phrase of the hymn. As accompaniment to the unison last verse, the first trumpet is assigned a countermelody, while the lower three parts duplicate much of the homophonic accompaniment of the organ, with the melody in the second trumpet and some additional embellishment in the lower brass. The optional use of timpani provides punctuation and, after the vocal entrance, reinforces the pedal point in the organ. The overall effect is a grand climax to this chorale concertato.

Jazz and Rock Styles

Most vocal jazz choirs rely exclusively upon a rhythm section (discussed in Chapter 15) for accompaniment, though increasingly wind instruments are being included. The instrumentation ranges from solo instruments to big band, but most published arrangements that include wind instruments call for three: high, medium, and low. The preferred combination is trumpet, alto saxophone, and trombone, because at a loud volume, the brass outer voices deliver a punch, while at a lower volume, a rather warm homogeneous sound is achievable. Trumpet, alto, and tenor saxophone is also a possible combination.

In a vocal jazz arrangement, the score setup is as follows (as illustrated in the examples below):

voices

wind instruments—according to tessitura; often on one treble clef staff (in concert pitch) if manageable; otherwise on separate staves with appropriate transpositions

rhythm section—piano/guitar
        bass (sometimes reading bass clef staff of piano part)
        drums (sometimes using a single-line staff)

In this style, the "horns" (as the wind instruments are called) usually work together in a homophonic rather than a contrapuntal texture. In a jazz setting, a pleasing mixture of unison and open and close voicings is desirable, with most three-note voicings including the third and seventh of the chord (and possibly one upper extension). The chord root is not usually included, to avoid a "bottom-heavy" sonority.

Example 16–5. Croft (arr. L. Sowerby): *O God, Our Help in Ages Past*

(Continued next page)

Example 16–6 illustrates various instrumental roles in this style. In the second measure, the instruments punctuate the vocal phrase with a widely-voiced, bright chord that falls off immediately. In the fourth and fifth bars, the horns double the voices to add weight to their phrase and to increase the contrast when *all* instruments drop out in the sixth bar. The instrumental silence reinforces the text (''stops'') and dramatically reduces the energy level for the phrase ending and return to the soft, relaxed feeling of the opening. In the seventh measure, the instruments fill by opening from a unison *d* and connecting the chorus's *d* with their *a* in the last measure. Again, the interest is in the variety of roles and voicings rather than in complex counterpoint. The relaxed nature of the song is enhanced by giving the instruments smooth lines in comfortable, ''warm'' registers.

In a rock setting, more horn unisons and triads are desirable for strength and simplicity, with high registers contributing a bright edge, as demonstrated in Example 16–7. Note, in measures 1–2 and 5–6 of the example, how intense, unison horn figures fill the space between vocal phrases, maintain the high energy level, and allow the piano to concentrate, with the rest of the rhythmn section, on a repetitive harmonic-rhythmic pattern. In the third and fourth measures, the horns (trumpet, alto saxophone, and trombone) change to syncopated triads to ''kick'' the vocal lines, but stay in the lower register until the next fill so as not to overpower the choir.

In both jazz and rock styles, the instruments can be featured for an entire section of an arrangement. One instrument might play an improvised or written-out solo, or all of the horns might play a written-out passage for ''soli.'' The singers may

Example 16–6. Spence, Keith, and Bergman (arr. D. Riley and D. Wilson): *Nice 'n' Easy*

Example 16–7. Anka and Harris (arr. K. Shaw): *Jubilation*

be *tacet* during that section, may sing background figures (on "ooh," etc.) appropriate to the style, or may interact with the soloists. Some sort of choral involvement is recommended so that the singers maintain their interest in the performance and do not have to just "stand there" for an extended period. Example 16-8 illustrates interaction between instruments and choir in such a passage.

Arrangements of rock songs tend to have instruments play repetitive figures throughout in order to contribute to the hypnotic drive of the music. However, if the horns are featured, their lines often provide a virtuosic display, playing primarily in unison for strength but opening to chords for punctuating figures. In a rock setting, these intricate lines might be doubled in the guitar, keyboard, or bass parts. Such a passage is illustrated in Example 16–9.

In both jazz and rock styles, the task of the horns is usually to contribute to the arrangement's growth. A common plan is as follows:

Introduction—all instruments or just rhythm section

First section—no horns

Second section—sparse horn fills

Third section—horn reinforcement of vocal parts plus fills

Fourth section—horn solo

Fifth (and later) section—important, quasi-independent horn role (counterlines, dramatic fills, vocal doubling)

Example 16–8. Spence, Keith, and Bergman (arr. D. Riley and D. Wilson): *Nice 'n' Easy*

Example 16–9.

It is important to remember that regardless of the shape of the arrangement or size of the choral or instrumental ensemble, the work is essentially choral and the instrumental writing must not overwhelm the choral writing—in dynamics, interest, or complexity. With this kept in mind, an arrangement with a conventional or unconventional instrumental ensemble can cause the source material to flower in a unique way, and can be a dramatic addition to a program.

CHAPTER SEVENTEEN

GETTING YOUR
ARRANGEMENT PUBLISHED

CHORAL ARRANGEMENTS ARE PUBLISHED AS THE RESULT of one of two procedures. First, a publisher who owns the "rights" to a song (permission to publish an arrangement of source material not in the public domain) may commission a recognized composer-arranger to arrange the song for a specified combination of voices and instruments. Second, anyone may submit an original arrangement to a publisher for consideration. This discussion will focus upon the second procedure for obvious reasons.

PREPARATION OF THE MANUSCRIPT

The manuscript to be submitted to a publisher need not be copied professionally, but it must be musically accurate, properly notated, neat, and clearly legible—in dark pencil, if not in ink. *A cappella* arrangements should have a piano part (with the indication "for rehearsal only") which duplicates the vocal lines in the correct octave.

It is preferable that a good photocopy on standard-sized (8½ X 11 in.) paper be submitted rather than the original, so that the arranger can make future changes on the original if necessary. Obviously, the more accurate and neat the manuscript, the better the initial impression on the publisher.

SELECTING A PUBLISHER

Before a publisher can consider an arrangement for publication, it must be determined whether the source material is in the *public domain*, meaning, legally available to anyone for use. Such material usually includes traditional folk songs, patriotic songs, hymn tunes, and the like. Songs written in this century may well be protected by copyright, meaning that a publisher can only publish an arrangement of such songs if permission is granted by the copyright owner to do so. Therefore, before submitting an arrangement of copyrighted material (and perhaps before writing the arrangement), it would be important to determine whether a publisher can obtain such permission.

Secondly, a publisher should be selected according to the style, nature, and vocal combination of the arrangement. Most publishing houses publish material according to a prescribed market or general company policy, and this is reflected in the type of arrangements they publish consistently. Therefore, a study of a given company's catalogue will determine whether they might be receptive to a particular arrangement, and will avoid the very common mistake of submitting, for example, a pop arrangement for elementary school chorus to a company that specializes in sacred music for mature choirs. It is likely that a company that has published a few arrangements in a given style will take a serious look at one of a similar nature. Many people submit arrangements daily, making the competition keen, but companies are always looking for good new writers.[1]

Once the above investigation is complete, the following should accompany the manuscript itself:

1. A cover letter briefly explaining the nature of the arrangement (including its strong points and potential market), and an indication of your background, including titles, dates, and publishers of other arrangements to your credit.

2. A tape recording of the arrangement if available, even if not of the highest quality.

3. A self-addressed, stamped envelope for anything you would like returned. Do *not* send any material that is irreplaceable.

4. If you are submitting an original choral composition, a letter from the owner of any copyrighted text, granting permission for the text to be set in your arrangement and published in the manner that you anticipate from the publisher; of course, any text in the public domain, such as psalms or poems written previous to the twentieth century, will require no such letter, though it may be helpful to indicate to the publisher that the text is, in fact, in the public domain.

---

names and addresses of publishers, consult *The Musician's Guide*, 6th ed. (Chicago: Marquis edia, 1980).

The total package should be addressed to the choral editor of a given company, unless the name of the appropriate individual is known. The arrangement should be submitted to one company at a time, out of courtesy, and a month or so should be allowed to pass before a follow-up letter is appropriate. Editors are very busy, though at some point, you do want to call your arrangement to their attention.

If your work is accepted for publication, the publisher will send you a contract, including the terms of publication and remuneration. If your work is rejected, feel free to send it to two or three other companies before reevaluating the arrangement's potential. Sometimes an arrangement is rejected for reasons of quality or general marketability, but sometimes it may be attractive to one company while another does not find it appropriate for their catalogue. Of course, having an arrangement accepted is the objective of this procedure, but rejection can also prove instructive. It is appropriate to ask a publisher the basis of rejection, for an editor's expertise can lend insight into such things as suitability of the text, level of difficulty, and overall effectiveness of the arrangement.

USE OF COPYRIGHTED MATERIAL FOR PERFORMANCE AND PUBLICATION

It is helpful to know certain distinctions with regard to the use of copyrighted material in performance and publication, as well as specific information concerning the obtaining of permission to use such material.

Whether, and by whom, certain source material is protected under copyright can be determined by contacting the U.S. Copyright Office in Washington, D.C., or often by contacting one of the performing rights organizations: American Society of Composers, Artists, and Publishers (ASCAP), Broadcast Music, Inc. (BMI), or the Society of European Stage Authors and Composers (SESAC—which licenses a more specialized collection). All are based in New York City.

Performance Rights

If only permission to perform copyrighted source material is desired, the arranger should write to the copyright owner with details of the arrangement (vocal and instrumental combination, length, etc.) and of projected performance plans (number and settings of performances, whether—and how much—admission will be charged, nature of the performing group, etc.). The owner, if consenting, will send permission to use the material *gratis*, or for a fee, usually dependent upon the scope and nature of performance plans.

Publications Rights

If the arrangement is being written for submission to a publisher for consideration, permission need not be granted by the copyright owner in advance, but the publisher must have access to the rights as discussed above. An arranger may copyright an arrangement of source material that is original or in the public domain, or of copyrighted source material for which permission has been granted in writing by the copyright owner. This is done by sending a copy of the manuscript, the required copyright registration form, and fee, to the Copyright Office at the Library of Congress, Washington, D.C. 20559. However, a publisher will automatically copyright any arrangement accepted for publication.[2]

---

[2]For more detailed information regarding copyright, consult *This Business of Music*, by Sidney Shemel and M. William Krasilovsky (Paul Ackerman, ed.; New York: Billboard Publications, Inc., 1977).

APPENDIX I

MELODIC SOURCE MATERIAL FOR ARRANGING

TRADITIONAL-FOLK

All the Pretty Little Horses

Hush - a - bye, don't you cry, Go to sleep - y, lit - tle ba - by.
When you wake you shall have All the pret - ty lit - tle

hors - es. Blacks and grays, Dap - ples and bays, Coach and four - a lit - tle

hors - es. Hush - a - bye, don't you cry, Go to sleep-y, lit - tle ba - by.

Aura Lee

1. As the black-bird in the spring, 'Neath the wil-low tree ___
Sat and pip'd, I heard him sing, Sing of Au-ra Lee.
Au-ra Lee! Au-ra Lee! Maid of gold-en hair!
Sun-shine came a-long with thee, And swal-lows in the air.

Gypsy Rover

The gyp-sy rov-er came o-ver the hill, Bound thru the val-ley so
shad-y; He whis-tled and he sang till the green woods rang, And
he won the heart of a la - dy. ___

Refrain

Lah-dee - o, lah-dee - o-ah-day, Lah-dee - o, lah-dee -
ay - dee. He whis-tled and he sang till the green woods rang, And
he won the heart of a la - dy.

I Know Where I'm Going

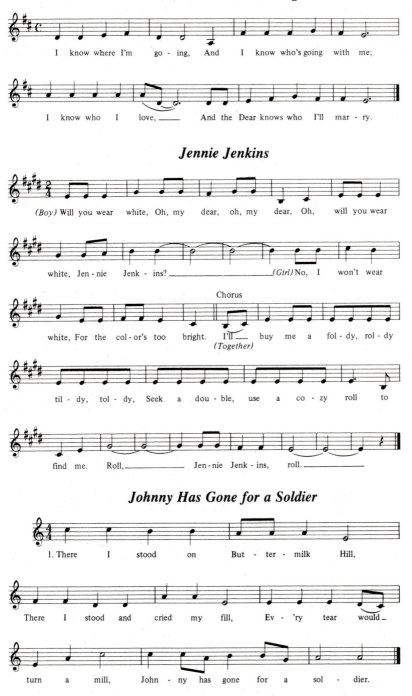

I know where I'm go - ing, And I know who's going with me;

I know who I love, ____ And the Dear knows who I'll mar - ry.

Jennie Jenkins

(Boy) Will you wear white, Oh, my dear, oh, my dear, Oh, will you wear

white, Jen - nie Jenk - ins? _____ *(Girl)* No, I won't wear

Chorus

white, For the col - or's too bright. I'll __ buy me a fol - dy, rol - dy
(Together)

til - dy, tol - dy, Seek a dou - ble, use a co - zy roll to

find me. Roll, _____ Jen - nie Jenk - ins, roll. _____

Johnny Has Gone for a Soldier

1. There I stood on But - ter - milk Hill,

There I stood and cried my fill, Ev - 'ry tear would __

turn a mill, John - ny has gone for a sol - dier.

Magic Penny

Love is some - thing if you give it a - way, __ give it a - way, __
give it a - way. __ Love is some - thing if you give it a - way, __ you

Fine

end up hav - ing more. It's just like a mag - ic pen - ny,

hold it tight and you won't have an - y, lend it, spend __ it, and you'll

D.C. al Fine

have so man - y they'll roll all o - ver the floor, for

My Horses Ain't Hungry

1. My hors - es ain't hun - gry, they won't eat your hay, __
__ So fare - thee - well Pol - ly, I'm
go - ing a - way. __ Your par - ents don't
like me, they say I'm too poor, They __ say I'm not
wor - thy to en - ter your door. __

Shenandoah

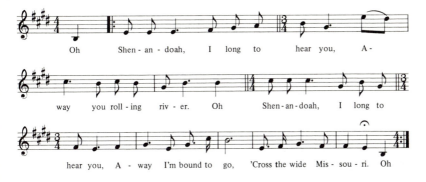

Oh Shen - an - doah, I long to hear you, A-
way you roll - ing riv - er. Oh Shen - an - doah, I long to
hear you, A - way I'm bound to go, 'Cross the wide Mis - sou - ri. Oh

The Water Is Wide

The wa-ter is wide, _____ I can't get o'er. Nei-ther have
I _____ the wings to ___ fly. Oh, go and
get _____ me a lit - tle ___ boat, And we both shall
row, my true love and ___ I. _____

SPIRITUALS

Kumbaya

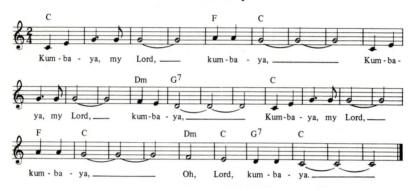

Kum - ba - ya, my Lord, ____ kum - ba - ya, _____ Kum - ba - ya, my Lord, ____ kum-ba - ya, _____ Kum-ba - ya, my Lord, ____ kum - ba - ya, _____ Oh, Lord, kum - ba - ya. _____

Oh, Sinner Man

Oh, sin - ner man, where you gon - na run to; Oh, sin - ner man, where you gon - na run to; Oh, sin - ner man, where you gon - na run to, All on that day? ____

This Little Light of Mine

Chorus:
This lit - tle light of mine, ___ I'm gon - na let it shine._

___ This lit - tle light of mine, _____

I'm gon - na let it shine. _____ This lit - tle light of mine,_

___ I'm gon - na let it shine, ___ Ev - 'ry

day, ev - 'ry way, Ev - 'ry day, ev - 'ry

way, ___ gon - na let my lit - tle light shine. _____

This Train

1. This train is bound for glo - ry, this train, _____

This train is bound for glo - ry, this train, _____

This train is bound for glo - ry, Car - ries none but the

good and ho - ly, This train is bound for glo - ry, this train. _____

Wade In the Water

Were You There?

SACRED

Coventry Carol

1. Lul - ly, lul - lay, thou lit - tle ti - ny child, By, by, lul -
ly, lul - lay. ____ Lul - lay, thou lit - tle ti - ny
child, By, by, lul - ly, lul - lay. ____

O Little Town of Bethlehem

1. O lit - tle town of Beth - le - hem, How still we__ see thee lie, A -
bove thy deep and dream - less sleep The si - lent __ stars go by. Yet
in thy dark streets shin - eth The ev - er - last - ing light, The
hopes and fears of all the years, Are met in thee to - night.

Glorious Things of Thee Are Spoken

AUSTRIAN HYMN. John Newton, 1725–1807. Franz Joseph Haydn, 1732–1809.

1. Glo - rious things of thee are spo - ken, Zi - on, cit - y of our God;
2. See, the streams of liv - ing wa - ters, Springing from e - ter - nal love,
3. Round each hab - i - ta - tion hov - ering, See the cloud and fire ap - pear

He whose word can - not be bro - ken Formed thee for His own a - bode;
Well sup - ply thy sons and daugh - ters, And all fear of want re - move;
For a glo - ry and a cov - ering, Show - ing that the Lord is near!

On the Rock of A - ges found - ed, What can shake thy sure re - pose?
Who can faint, while such a riv - er Ev - er flows their thirst to assuage?
Glo - rious things of thee are spo - ken, Zi - on, city of our God;

With sal - va - tion's walls sur-round - ed, Thou mayst smile at all thy foes.
Grace which like the Lord, the Giv - er, Nev - er falls from age to age.
He, whose word can - not be bro - ken, Formed thee for His own a - bode.

Praise Ye the Lord, the Almighty

(Lobe Den Herren) Joachim Neander, 1650–1680. Trans. by Catherine Winkworth, 1829–1878. "Stralsund Gesangbuch," 1665. Arr. in "Praxis Pietatis Melica," 1668.

PARTICULARLY ADAPTABLE TO
POPULAR STYLES

As Time Goes By

H. Hupfeld

You must re-mem-ber this, a kiss is still a kiss, A sigh is just a sigh;
when two lov-ers woo, they still say,"I love you," On this you can re-ly,

The fun-da-men-tal things ap-ply, as time goes by. ——— And
No mat-ter what the fu-ture brings as time goes by. ———

by.   Moon-light and love— songs nev-er out of date, Hearts full of pas-sion,

jeal-ou-sy and hate, Wom-an needs man— and man must have his mate, That

no one can de-ny. It's still the same old sto-ry, the fight for love and glo-ry, A

case of do or die.   The world will al-ways wel-come lov-ers, As time goes by.

Autumn Leaves

Mercer & Kosma

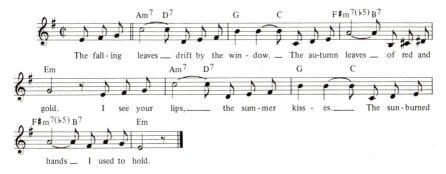

The fall-ing leaves __ drift by the win - dow. __ The au-tumn leaves __ of red and
gold. I see your lips, ____ the sum - mer kiss - es. ____ The sun - burned
hands __ I used to hold.

© 1947 Ardmore Music. Reprinted by permission of Morley
Music.

Darlin' Corey

Wake __ up, wake up, dar - lin' Cor - ey, ____
____ What makes you sleep __ so __ sound?
The ____ rev - e - nue of - fi - cers is a - com - in' ____
__ To __ tear your still __ house __ down.

Every Night When the Sun Goes In

I Could Write a Book

Rodgers/Hart

© 1941 Chappell and Co. Reprinted by permission of Hal Leonard Publishing Co.

Tom Dooley

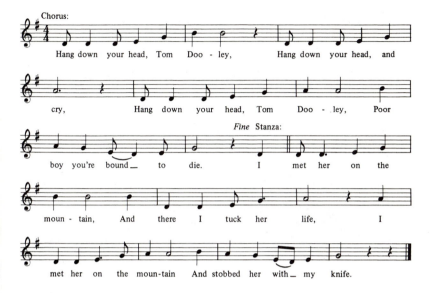

Chorus: Hang down your head, Tom Doo - ley, Hang down your head, and cry, Hang down your head, Tom Doo - ley, Poor boy you're bound — to die. I met her on the moun - tain, And there I tuck her life, I met her on the moun-tain And stobbed her with — my knife.

APPENDIX II

COMPLETE CHORAL ARRANGEMENTS FOR STUDY

Early in the Morning

3-part Mixed Voices

Words by Mary Kay Beall

Arranged by John Carter

Goin' to Boston

Three Part Mixed Choir

American Folk Song

Arranged by Harry Wilson
and Walter Ehret

From Harry Wilson and Walter Ehret, *Prentice-Hall Choral Series,* Book 2 (Englewood Cliffs, N.J. 1960), pp. 44–51. Reprinted by permission of the publisher.

Let There Be Peace on Earth

Soprano and Alto

By Sy Miller and Jill Jackson   Arranged by Hawley Ades

*The larger number is preferable when the chorus is large.

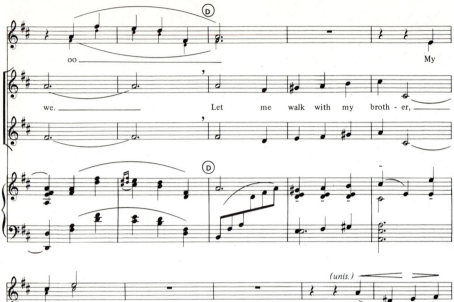

oo _____

we. _____ Let me walk with my broth - er, _____

My

broth - er, oo _____ *(unis.)*

In per - fect har - mo - ny. _____

(Small group joins chorus)
Soprano *mf*

Let peace be-

Alto *mf*

Let peace be - gin with me, Let

_____
*Small notes are optional.

288

take each mo-ment and live each mo-ment In peace e - ter - nal-
ly. ___ Let there be peace on earth, And
let it be - gin with me! ___ Let it be - gin with me! ___

*Small notes are optional.

**Voices for which large notes are low, use small notes.

Nice 'N' Easy

SATB, 3 horns and rhythm section

Music by Lew Spence
Lyric by Marilyn Keith
and Alan Bergman

Arranged by Dave Riley
and Dana Wilson

Sing a Rainbow

Two-part voices

Words and Music
by Arthur Hamilton

Arranged by John Coates, Jr.

---

*s.a., t. b., or a chorus of changed, changing, and unchanged voices. In the latter, changed and changing voices sing Part I an octave lower than written and unchanged voices sing Part II where written.

Complete Choral Arrangements for Study

Swansea Town

SATB

Arranged by Gustav Holst

on,   The   night   so dark   as   an - y - thing,   we__ can - not   see   the

moon;   Our__ good old   ship   she__ is   toss'd aft,   our   rig - ging   is__   all__

INDEX

Parallel style writing, 22, 147, 162
Parlando, 176
Partner songs, in two-part-texture, 74
Permission to publish (*See* Copyrighted material)
Piano (*see also* "rhythm section"), notation, 13–14; score setup, 8; technical considerations, 44–45
Pop music, accompaniment, 236; vocal styles, 220–21
Primary triads, 23, 24, 25
Publisher, selecting, 252
Pyramid, 180–82

*Q*uodlibet, in two-part texture, 74

*R*epeats, score setup, 10
Rests, 13
Rhythm section, in larger instrumental ensemble, 244–50; instruments, 224–35; score setup, 8
Rock ballad, 219; accompaniment, 234
Rock music, accompaniment, 231–33; endings, 219–20; harmonies, 215, 217; melodic inflections, 217; rhythm, 217; scales (*see also* Scales, jazz), 215; sources and description, 214–15
Round, in two-part texture, 70–72

*S*A, adapted from SATB, 184; characteristics, 59
SAB, adapted from SATB, 184; characteristics, 124, 125, 127–30, 133, 135, 137, 139
Sacred setting, animated homophony in, 127, 129; beginning, 109; countermelody in, 133; ending, 109; figuration in, 135, 156, 157; hymn, 64, 151, 154, 243; imitation in, 70–71, 139, 142, 160, 161; instrumental accompaniment (*see also* Organ), 243–44; note-against-note in, 145; ostinato in, 156, 158; planning complete arrangement, 121–23; SSAA, 162, 163, 164; TTBB, 164, 165, 166, 167, 168
Scales, harmonic minor, 23; jazz, 23, 194, 198, 215
Scat syllables (*See under* Neutral syllables)
SCB, 124
Score setup, 6–11
Secondary triads, 23, 24, 25

Seventh chords, diatonic, 25–27; secondary dominant, 27
Shuffle, 229
Slides, in barbershop style, 165–67
Speaking, 176–77
SSA, 124, 125, 135, 139
SSAA, 144–45, 162, 163, 164
Stemming, 12–13, 239
String ensemble, score setup, 8
"Sweet Adelines," 162, 165–67
Swing, four-beat ("straight ahead") style, 194–211, 227; rhythm, 187, 188, 211; two-beat style, 194–211, 227

*T*ags (*see also* Endings), in barbershop quartet style, 165–67
Tempo (*See* Form delineation)
Tempo markings, in jazz styles, 192, 211
Tessitura, 4, 76
Text, capturing the mood of, 31; notation, 14–16
Text treatment, in countermelody, 61, 133, 151; declamation, 16–17; in endings, 105, 106, 109, 112; in figuration, 66, 135, 155; in imitation, 156, 158; in introduction, 101; in melody line with background vocal texture, 130, 133, 151; in note-against-note texture, 145; in ostinato, 68–70, 137, 156; in planning the arrangement, 116, 122
Texture (*See* Form delineation)
Triadic harmony, 23
Tritone substitution, 201
TTBB, 144–45, 162–67; adapted from SATB, 184, 186
Two-beat style (*See* Swing)

*V*oice leading, 148; diminished intervals, 21; tendency tones, 20–21
Voicing (*see also* Chord, Jazz), close, 18–19, 147, 162; mixed, 19; open, 18–19, 147

*W*altz, 49; jazz, 191